D1527348

READY TO GIVE AN ANSWER

A Catechism of Reformed Distinctives

> But sanctify the Lord God in your hearts: and be ready always to give an answer to every man that asketh you a reason of the hope that is in you with meekness and fear.
>
> I Peter 3:15

Herman Hoeksema · Herman Hanko

Reformed Free Publishing Association
4949 Ivanrest Avenue, S.W.
Grandville, MI 49418-9709

REFORMED FREE PUBLISHING ASSOC.
4949 Ivanrest Avenue
Grandville, MI 49418-9709

Library of Congress Catalog Number:
97-075394

ISBN 0-916206-58-0

Printed in the United States of America

Protestant Reformed ministers pictured on the cover:

1   John A. Heys (1910-   )
2   Marinus Schipper (1906-1985)
3   Herman Veldman (1908-1997)
4   Herman Hoeksema (1886-1965)
5   Cornelius Hanko (1907-   )
6   George M. Ophoff (1891-1962)
7   Homer C. Hoeksema (1923-1989)
8   George C. Lubbers (1909-   )
9   Henry H. Kuiper (1905-1961)
10 Gerrit Vos (1894-1968)

Cover artwork:
Jeff Steenholdt

This book is gratefully dedi-
cated to the memory of our
spiritual fathers who have
fought a good fight, have
now finished the course, and
have kept the faith.
                    —II Timothy 4:7

Preface

Rev. Herman Hoeksema's book, *The Protestant Reformed Churches in America,* has long been out of print. As those who are acquainted with it will remember, it was composed of two parts: a detailed history of the events surrounding 1924 which became the occasion for the organization of the Protestant Reformed Churches; and an invaluable "catechism," which expounded the doctrinal issues involved in that common grace controversy.

A Watered Garden, written more recently by Gertrude Hoeksema, covers the history of the Protestant Reformed Churches from the beginning of their history to the time the book was written — about a decade ago. Because *The Protestant Reformed Churches in America* was limited to only one part of that history, it was not reprinted after Gertrude Hoeksema's book came out. However, the Reformed Free Publishing Association believes that especially the last section of *The Protestant Reformed Churches in America* is too important a part of our heritage to permit it to be lost. They decided therefore to republish that part of the book, so that Herman Hoeksema's own careful analysis of the issues of 1924 would be once more available.

To enhance the value of such a re-publication, it was decided, also, to add another section, in similar, question-and-answer format, dealing with the doctrinal issues involved in the controversy of 1953. The focus of this latter section would therefore be the doctrinal questions which occupied the PRC during those difficult days when they lost over half their membership.

It is my hope and prayer that this treatment of the doctrinal questions which so emphatically shaped the life of our churches will be a help in preserving the precious heritage which God has entrusted to our care and will assist those who read and study it to "give an answer to those who ask" them concerning their faith.

The catechetical format was used in the presentation of the doctrinal issues of 1953 to make it similar in format to the first section. This format should also be of practical benefit for ministers who desire to use the material in societies, catechism classes, and other Bible study meetings.

At the suggestion of the publishers, I have included in the book a brief history of the controversies of 1924 and 1953. This history is not intended to take the place of the more detailed history found in *A Watered Garden;* its purpose is rather to give a readily accessible and handy summary of the history to serve as the background for the catechism section.

I wish to acknowledge the helpful suggestions made by my colleagues in the seminary, Profs. Decker and Engelsma. My father, who lived through the controversies of 1924 and 1953 and was minister in First Protestant Reformed Church in 1953, has read the manuscript and has offered many excellent suggestions. Mr. Don Doezema has also read the manuscript and has given many suggestions on the formal aspects of the writing. To all these men I express my gratitude.

I have taken the liberty to make small editorial changes in the material of Rev. Herman Hoeksema in a few places where the meaning seemed to be obscure.

The heritage of the Reformed faith which God has given to us is precious. May this book serve to encourage us to be faithful to it.

Herman Hanko
October, 1997

CONTENTS

Section I

The History

Herman Hanko

The History

The history of the Protestant Reformed Churches cannot be properly understood unless the formation of this denomination is considered to be a true reformation of the church of Christ in America. Herman Hoeksema, himself one of the founders of the Protestant Reformed Churches, insisted on this. About six years after the denomination was formed, he wrote:

> It will serve to shed the proper light upon the origin of the Protestant Reformed Churches, which is not to be viewed as a deplorable, accidental but unavoidable result of the Janssen controversy, but as a *reformation* of the churches, a return from the erroneous and dangerous path of common grace to the fundamentally Reformed line of the Synod of Dordrecht as drawn in the three forms of unity (*The Protestant Reformed Churches in America*, p. 25).

While Hoeksema wrote these words to describe the relation between the so-called Janssen controversy (an important event which we will discuss a bit later) and the common grace struggle, he wrote very emphatically that the movement resulting in the Protestant Reformed Churches (PRC) must be understood as church reformation in the same sense in which church reformation had taken place in the past.

The justification for describing the origin of the PRC as church reformation lies in the fact that crucially important doctrinal issues were involved, issues which not only occupied the church's attention in the 1920's, but were in fact at the heart of the great controversies that have raged in the church from the time of Augustine.

The doctrinal question put in its most basic form was: Is the grace of Almighty God common to all men, or is it particular and for the elect alone?

Yet, as the controversy of 1924 soon showed, other issues were implied. Some of these were: Does God love all men, or does He love only His elect? Is He merciful to everyone, or only to His own people? Does His kindness come to every man whether he be wicked or righteous, or only to those whom He has chosen in Christ?

Still other questions were involved. Does God desire to save all men, or does He will to save only some? And if He desires to save all (which common grace affirms), does He make salvation available to all through a Christ that died for all, so that salvation depends upon the choice of man's free will? Or is salvation the work of God alone — a work which He performs for His elect by the irresistible operations of the Spirit in the heart?

It all finally comes down to this one question: Is God sovereign in salvation? Or is man powerful enough to resist God and to determine his own destiny?

These, as anyone can readily see, are crucial questions. In fact, it is not an exaggeration to say that since the time when the Synod of Chalcedon settled the doctrine of the person and natures of Christ in 451, most of the controversies in the church have been over these questions.

These were the issues in the fifth century between Augustine, Bishop of Hippo, and Pelagius, a monk from Britain. Pelagius taught an inherent goodness of man, an ability of man to choose for the good apart from grace, and a love of God for all men. Augustine defended the doctrines of sovereign and double predestination, total depravity, and particular and sovereign grace in the work of salvation.

These same issues surfaced in the ninth century when the Roman Catholic Church, in the interests of preserving the idea of the meritorious value of good works, killed Gottschalk. Gottschalk had valiantly defended the views of Augustine, which he saw to be the teachings of Scripture, and which he attempted to restore to the confession of the church.

When Luther nailed his theses on the chapel door at Wittenburg and so launched the Reformation, he did so in the defense of the great truth that justification is by faith alone, and not by faith plus works, as Rome taught. And when Calvin thundered the truth from Geneva in a voice heard throughout Europe and down through the centuries, he made his central starting point *Soli Deo Gloria*, for he taught, over against Rome's Pelagianism, that God is sovereign in all His works and ways.

The Canons of Dordrecht, one of the great Reformation creeds, was written in defense of eternal predestination, total depravity, limited atonement, irresistible grace, and the preservation of the saints. It is thus the confession of the Reformed churches throughout Europe over against the Arminian conception of things which, in making grace common, taught conditional predestination, partial depravity, universal atonement, resistible grace, and the falling away of saints. Nor was Dordt afraid to identify Arminianism with Pelagianism, and to describe Pelagianism as out of hell. (See Canons II, B, 3, 6; III & IV, A, 2, 10, B, 7, 9; V, B, 2.)

These same issues were on the foreground in that reformation of the Dutch churches in the 19th century when the Reformed Church in the Netherlands was formed under the leadership of Hendrik DeCock and Abraham Kuyper.

The battle of faith which is fought through the ages is a battle in defense of the sovereignty of God in the work of the salvation of His elect people in Jesus Christ, over against salvation dependent on man's free will.

The issue was essentially the same in 1924 when the PRC began.

Stated in starkest terms, the doctrinal issue in 1924, when the PRC began, was the issue of common vs. particular grace. This doctrinal question did not, so to speak, arise out of the blue. It had a history.

A brief look at that history will help to set the controversy over common grace in its correct light.

The Christian Reformed Church (CRC) was formed as a separate denomination in 1857, when immigrants from the Netherlands settled in the area of what is now Holland, Michigan. Most of these immigrants were, in the Netherlands, members of the churches of the Separation (*De Afscheiding*), the reformatory movement led by Hendrik DeCock.

While DeCock was himself a staunch defender of the doctrines of sovereign grace, some of the men who left the apostate state church (Hervormde Kerk) with him were not as strong as he. Because the people of the Separation were, through immigration, the founders of the CRC, the weakness of the Separation soon appeared also in the CRC. Herman Hoeksema writes:

> Even before this time (1918), it must be recorded, the Christian Reformed Churches had never been wholly purged from the leaven of Pelagianism and Arminianism. The churches were, indeed, officially Reformed, united on the basis of the three forms of unity as their standards, but the actual condition was by no means in full accord with this official stand. The error of two irreconcilable wills of God, according to which, on the one hand, God willed that all men should be saved, while, on the

other hand, He had predestinated His own
from before the foundation of the world
and reprobated the others, had found a
ready acceptance in the churches. So deeply
had the error, that the gospel of salvation is
a well-meaning offer of grace on the part of
God to all men, struck root, and so generally was it accepted as Reformed truth, that
it had become the general tenor of preaching and instruction, that it was openly and
officially taught in the Theological School
of the Christian Reformed Churches, and
that denial of this evident error was considered a dangerously extreme or one-sided
view, if not a downright heresy (*The Protestant Reformed Churches* . . . , pp. 14, 15).

Along with such Arminian errors, Hoeksema found in
the churches "a gradually growing spirit of confessional
indifferentism," a "falsely conceived 'broad-mindedness'
together with the manifestation of a spirit of worldly-
mindedness, that would hide behind the name of 'Calvinism,'" and a "latitudinarian" spirit which "opposed the
antithesis, stood for a 'broader' view of the Christian's life
and calling in the world, and strove to bridge the gap
between the world and the Church" (*The Protestant Reformed Churches* . . . , pp. 15, 16).

The part of the reformatory movement in the Netherlands that had been led by Dr. Abraham Kuyper also
made itself felt in this country. Sad to say, Kuyper's
emphasis on the sovereignty of grace in salvation rooted
in sovereign predestination was not the chief influence.
Rather, Kuyper's later development of common grace
was snatched up in the CRC. Again, Hoeksema informs
us that the latitudinarian party "discovered that [Kuyper's]
theory of common grace offered them a philosophy that

would support their latitudinarian views in the name of Calvinism" (*The Protestant Reformed Churches . . .* , p. 16).

A case arose in the CRC which forced the question of common grace on the attention of the churches. The case involved Dr. Ralph Janssen, a very learned and scholarly professor of Old Testament in Calvin Theological Seminary. Educated in some of the outstanding universities in Europe, Dr. Janssen had become persuaded of the value of higher critical studies of Scripture. In his classroom instruction he explained the Old Testament from a higher critical viewpoint.

Dr. Janssen's higher critical approach to Scripture led him to some positions which his colleagues and fellow professors in the seminary challenged. He taught that not every book in the Old Testament canon was truly canonical, but that the canonicity of a book had to be determined by empirical methods. He was of the opinion that much of the religion of the patriarchs and the nation of Israel was gained from the religions of the heathen nations with which the Jews had contact. This position, in turn, led him to deny that every event recorded in the Old Testament was historical. The exploits of Samson, e.g., were likely legends imitating the hero-legends of other nations. He was personally persuaded of the so-called documentary theory of the Pentateuch, a higher critical theory which claimed that Moses did not write the first five books of the Bible, but that these books were composed by different authors, some from very late periods in Israel's history.

What was particularly disturbing to many in the church was his idea of miracles. Janssen firmly believed that the miracles in general had to be explained in keeping with conclusions of modern science. He gave to many of the miracles, therefore, a natural explanation. He explained, e.g., one of the Old Testament's most beautiful miracles, referred to in the New Testament as well, in a purely natural way. When Israel was without water in the wilderness on their way to Canaan, God brought water out of the rock for them through the command of Moses. Janssen refused to believe that God prepared that water for Israel in a miraculous fashion. The water was there all the time, Janssen said. Moses happened to hit a thin piece of rock which broke under his blow to release the water that was present. The miracle, if there was one at all, consisted in the rather providential coincidence of Moses hitting a thin place in the rock. This natural explanation had to be correct, so Janssen insisted, because science had proved that the amount of matter and energy in the universe is stable and constant, and, therefore, God would not create anything which had not been present in the universe from the beginning.

In this way the heart of the miracle was denied, for the New Testament points us to the fact that Christ is the Rock (I Cor. 10:1-4), and that the water which comes from Him is the Spirit who quenches our thirst eternally (John 7:37-39).

What was of particular interest in the matter was Janssen's appeal to the doctrine of common grace in support of his teachings. His appeal to the doctrine of common grace involved two points. In the first place, he defended his view that the Hebrew people of the Old Testament borrowed from pagan religions in forming their own monotheism on the ground that common grace, operative in all men, was capable of producing in the heathen truths which could be incorporated into the Hebrew religion without doing violence to this religion. And in the second place, he argued that modern science was also the fruit of common grace, and our interpretation of Scripture's miracles (including creation) had to fit the findings of modern science.

In the early stages of the controversy the synod of the CRC, meeting in June of 1920, exonerated Dr. Janssen and cleared him from charges of heresy. But little investigation was actually made, and the decision did not satisfy Janssen's seminary colleagues who had brought the original complaint.

At about the same time Rev. Hoeksema had obtained a large number of student notes and, after a personal study of these notes, came to the conclusion that Dr. Janssen was indeed guilty of teaching views contrary to Scripture and the Reformed confessions. In his column in the *Banner*, Rev. Hoeksema began analyzing Janssen's views and writing against them. It was also during this time that Hoeksema subjected Kuyper's views of common grace to the scrutiny of Scripture and the Reformed confessions and came to the conclusion that Kuyper was very wrong in his teachings on this subject.

As the case continued to plague the churches, the controversy grew in importance. The church papers were filled with writings about it; the Theological School Committee, responsible for the operation of the seminary, was bombarded with protests and overtures; a committee was appointed by the Theological School Committee to investigate the matter; and it all finally came to the synod of 1922 for adjudication.

The study committee appointed by the Theological School Committee was composed of seven members, three of whom supported Dr. Janssen, and four of whom were convinced his views were wrong. The result was a divided report on the floor of the synod. Rev. Hoeksema was a member of this committee, a part of the majority, and responsible for most of the work.

After the synod had carefully considered both reports, the views of the majority were adopted by the synod and Dr. Janssen was condemned. His tenure at the seminary was discontinued. The church, in its broadest gathering, condemned the higher critical views of one of its seminary professors.

What is of particular interest in the whole case is the fact that the doctrine of common grace, which Dr. Janssen had used as his weapon of defense, was never officially discussed. It does not appear in either the majority or the minority reports of the study committee; it was not discussed on the floor of the synod as an integral part of the case; and no mention of it was made in the official decisions of synod.

The reasons for this omission are not clear. Everyone involved in the case knew of the importance Dr. Janssen had given to common grace. And everyone also knew that the whole question of common grace was a burning issue in the churches. Perhaps both the committee that studied the material of Janssen and brought recommendations to the synod of 1922 and the synod itself feared that a discussion of common grace would tear the churches to pieces.

Hoeksema later regretted that common grace had not been immediately discussed and its scriptural and confessional basis examined. He wrote:

> In the light of subsequent history it was evidently a mistake on the part of the Reverends H. Danhof and H. Hoeksema, that they co-operated with the four professors (Dr. Janssen's colleagues, HH) in the Janssen controversy, rather than to oppose his views separately and from their own standpoint; that, for practical reasons, they allowed the deepest principles involved to be pushed into the background and the controversy to be confined to surface questions and differences (*The Protestant Reformed Churches* ..., p. 24).

Common grace, though ignored by the official bodies

in the church, was nevertheless given center place in
subsequent years. In fact, so soon after the Janssen
controversy did the issue of common grace reappear, that
two years later the same synod that had condemned Dr.
Janssen, now condemned Rev. Hoeksema for his denial of
common grace.

It is not always clear from the historical record why
the issue of common grace was forced so soon on the
attention of the churches. Partly the problem was that
many supporters of Dr. Janssen remained in the church
even when Dr. Janssen was expelled; and they were all
defenders of common grace, as Janssen had been. Even
some of those who opposed Dr. Janssen believed in
common grace in one form or another, although they
were not always clear on precisely what common grace
was.

At any rate, while Rev. Hoeksema was minister in the
Eastern Ave. CRC in Grand Rapids, Michigan, various
objections were lodged against his preaching and writing
because he denied the existence of common grace. Some
objections were lodged by members of his own congregation; some objections came from different parts of the
denomination. Eventually many of them found their way
to synod, which began its meetings on June 18, 1924.

The synod was inescapably confronted with the question of common grace. It could, of course, (and that may
have been the wise course of action to follow), postpone
action in order to give the churches time to study and
discuss the matter. But among some there was a certain
air of urgency, and the synod entered the whole subject at
once. After considerable discussion on the floor of the
synod, a lengthy statement concerning common grace
was adopted. (See *A Watered Garden*, where the decision
is quoted.)

A few remarks about the workings of the synod and
the final decision which was taken are in order.

The synod handled the whole matter of the protests and appeals against Hoeksema in a very unjust manner. Some of the protests were illegally on the floor of synod, but synod treated them in spite of their illegality. Hoeksema was denied the right of the floor and was not permitted to speak in his own defense. It is hard to imagine a greater miscarriage of justice. It is true that Hoeksema was not a delegate to the synod, but he was the one charged with false doctrine. Even in worldly courts a man charged with enormous crimes is given the right to a defense, either from his own lips or through another. But the synod of the CRC would not permit such a basic right to Hoeksema. The reasoning behind this is not easy to discover.

Finally, when Hoeksema solemnly promised that he would speak only once, the floor was given to him. Hoeksema used the opportunity to speak to a crowded church at an evening session to show the biblical and confessional basis for his denial of common grace. But this was the one and only time he spoke. When unjust and incorrect remarks were made subsequent to his defense, he was given no opportunity for rebuttal. And when he asked for the floor, he was dismissed with an airy reminder of his promise to speak but once.

In the final formulation of the doctrine of common grace, two ideas of common grace were brought together into one statement. The general grace of the well-meant offer of the gospel and a general attitude of favor on God's part towards all men were combined with the Kuyperian notion of the restraint of sin by the Holy Spirit and the good which unregenerate are capable of doing. Both ideas were present in the CRC. Both were included in the decision of 1924.

That the two ideas of common grace were brought together into one decision ought not to surprise us. After all, a grace of God which is common to all men, elect and reprobate alike, is a perversion of the gospel in whatever suit of clothes it wears. And whether that common grace comes to men in the preaching, or by a direct operation of the Spirit of Christ in the hearts of men, or through the good gifts of the creation which men receive from their Creator, or by a love of God for them all, it makes no essential difference. It remains a grace which never saves and never accomplishes its purpose.

Having dealt with the doctrine itself, synod faced also the question of what to do about Herman Hoeksema, who had made it very clear to synod that he did not then and would never agree to such a gross perversion of Scripture and the Reformed creeds.

The committee of pre-advice which presented synod with recommendations advised discipline. This was consistent and could be the only logical course of action for synod to follow. If common grace was, as synod claimed, the teaching of Scripture and the confessions, then it followed that Hoeksema, who openly informed synod that he would never subscribe to common grace, was guilty of militating against Scripture and the Reformed confessions. Reformed church polity is quite clear on the matter: such a person must be disciplined.

But synod did not quite have the courage for that. Although the recommendation of the committee of pre-advice was moved and supported, synod lacked the stomach to be consistent. Rather than pass a motion requiring censure, synod instead declared the very opposite: it officially pronounced Hoeksema as being fundamentally Reformed, but with this caveat: "though it be with an inclination to one-sidedness." The mystery of how synod could condemn a man's views as being contrary to Scripture and the confessions and yet pronounce him fundamentally Reformed remains to this day unsolved.

What synod was afraid to do, the classis to which

Herman Hoeksema's church belonged had the courage to do. Classis Grand Rapids East was confronted with the question of what to do with Hoeksema by appeals from members of Hoeksema's church, Eastern Ave. CRC. Although the classis met sporadically over the course of several months, the outcome was that both Rev. Herman Hoeksema and his consistory were required by the classis to subscribe wholeheartedly to the doctrine of common grace as formulated by the synod of 1924. When Eastern Ave's officebearers refused to do this because it violated their conscience before God, the classis proceeded to suspend Hoeksema from his office of minister of the Word of God and the sacraments, and that same classis declared the consistory to be outside the Christian Reformed Church.

The date was December 12, 1924.

Two other ministers and their consistories were also to experience the wrath of their classis.

Rev. Henry Danhof was pastor of First CRC in Kalamazoo, Michigan. He had been a delegate at the synod of the CRC which had adopted the Three Points of common grace. At the synod he had raised his objections to the doctrine and had let it be clearly known that he would never support such erroneous views. He and his congregation were a part of Classis Grand Rapids West.

Rev. George Ophoff was pastor of the Riverbend CRC in what is now Walker, Michigan. While Ophoff had not been present at the synod of 1924, he had expressed his convictions with regard to the Three Points of common grace by joining the staff of the *Standard Bearer.* This magazine had begun publication in October of 1924, partly because the pages of the official publication of the CRC, the *Banner,* were closed to Rev. Hoeksema, and partly because an organ was needed to inform the churches of the serious error the CRC had made at its synod. Rev. Ophoff had not only let his convictions be known by joining the staff of the *Standard Bearer*, but he had also clearly expressed himself on its pages in an early issue. Rev. Ophoff's congregation was also a part of Classis Grand Rapids West.

Classis Grand Rapids West was in no mood to dally. It wanted no discussion of the issues; it wanted no appeals to the next synod; it wanted no clarifications of the positions of Danhof and Ophoff. It simply required of these two men (and their consistories) that they submit without reservation to the decisions of the synod of 1924 with respect to common grace, or suffer deposition.

Those involved refused to submit. All were summarily deposed from office by official decision of the classis.

It was the beginning of the PRC.

True reformation in the church of Christ always involves a going back and a moving ahead. The going back is required because the denomination which needs reforming has become apostate and has moved away from what Jeremiah calls the "old paths." For this reason Jeremiah's admonition to Judah is always important in reformation: "Thus saith the Lord, Stand ye in the ways, and see, and ask for the old paths, where is the good way, and walk therein, and ye shall find rest for your souls" (6:16).

The old paths for the church of Christ in North America (as well as for Reformed churches throughout the world) were the paths of the Reformation of the 16th century with its sharp and unyielding emphasis on sovereign and particular grace. The old paths were the paths of the Synod of Dordt, which had emphatically repudiated the general grace of Arminianism, had charted the course of Reformed church polity, and had drawn up a confession which demonstrated beyond doubt that the teaching of God's grace for the elect only was the teaching of the Reformed churches from the beginning of their history.

This latter insistence of the Synod of Dordt (namely, that what it taught was the historic Reformed position) became evident in its statement that the Canons of Dordt were not to be construed as a *new* confession, but were a further explanation of some points of doctrine already contained in the Heidelberg Catechism and the Confession of Faith, both of which were official confessions of the Reformed churches of a half century earlier.

The activities of Classes Grand Rapids East and West showed that the church government of the denomination was also askew. Suspension and deposition of officebearers is a part of ecclesiastical censure of sin and an exercise of the keys of the kingdom of heaven. This task, as well as the preaching of the Word and the administration of the sacraments, belongs to the local consistories and not to broader ecclesiastical assemblies. For classes or synods to engage in discipline is the worst sort of hierarchy. Yet the CRC did not shrink from such hierarchy in order to rid itself of men who had been declared by the church itself to be Reformed, but who refused to agree to the false doctrine of common grace.

Faithful officebearers in the church of Christ, declared to be such by their own denomination, had been cruelly stripped of their offices, set naked on the street outside the doors of the church, and told to fend for themselves apart from the fellowship of the church.

And they were thus persecuted for no other reason than that they maintained the sovereignty and particularity of grace, a doctrine of the Reformed churches held since the days of John Calvin in Geneva.

A return to the "old paths," therefore, required also a return to the old true and tried Church Order of Dordrecht.

On March 6, 1925 the officebearers of the three congregations came together to form a new denomination. It was, in a sense, temporary, because all three congregations had appeals against the decisions of Classes Grand

Rapids East and West pending with the synod of 1926. Because of the temporary nature of their federation, they called themselves, "The Protesting Christian Reformed Churches." But no one held out any hope of the synod of 1926 retracting the erroneous doctrines of common grace, and no one expected the hierarchical decisions of two classes to be repudiated by synod. And so it proved to be.

Already the temporary "Act of Agreement" which was signed by the officebearers of the three congregations spoke of a return to the three forms of unity and the Church Order of Dordrecht.

The reformation was complete. The doctrines of free, sovereign, and particular grace were once again given free course, unencumbered by the burden of heresy. The autonomy of the local congregations was once again established on the basis of the Church Order of Dordrecht.

But a true reformation of the church of Christ is not and can never be merely a return to the "old paths." Within the church one cannot live in the past. One cannot dwell on past injustices nor fight battles long over.

This is not to say that the past is unimportant. The confession, worship, and government of the church of Christ throughout the ages are given the church by the Spirit of truth whom Christ promised to His church prior to His glorification (see John 14-16). The Spirit of truth guides the church into all truth. That means two things. It means, on the one hand, that the confession, worship, and government of the church of the past are the blessed fruit of the Spirit according to which the church must always live. But it also means that the work of the Spirit in the church is a continuing work, so that the Spirit, according to the Holy Scriptures which He Himself inspired, continues to reveal the truth in richer measure.

The church of Christ moves forward.

So it was with the PRC.

Some charged the PRC for existing only to inveigh

against and do battle with the evils of common grace. It was said that the PRC rode an old hobby horse, lived to criticize others, found its joy in chiding other denominations, and would disappear if it could no longer fight against common grace. This is not true.

Although indeed the PRC are compelled before God to show the evil of false doctrine, especially as it involves their own particular history, the churches have also moved forward by the guidance and direction of the Spirit of Christ.

Because the truth of sovereign and particular grace was the one great issue in the sad history of 1924, it was this truth which, emphasized in the churches, became the principle of further development of the truth within the churches.

Rev. Herman Hoeksema, rightly considered the spiritual father of the denomination, along with his colleague in the churches and in seminary, Rev. George Ophoff, made some distinctive contributions to what the church is called to believe.

It is not our purpose to go into these contributions in detail. But anyone acquainted with the many writings which have come from the pens of Hoeksema and Ophoff will know of the contributions to an understanding of sovereign grace which both of these men made in the *Standard Bearer* and other writings; and they will know how Herman Hoeksema made a significant and important contribution to the knowledge of the Reformed faith in his *Reformed Dogmatics.*

But if there is one doctrine which is a distinguishing truth of the PRC, it is the doctrine of God's eternal and unconditional covenant of grace. Firmly committed to the truth of sovereign and particular grace, and applying that truth to the biblically defined doctrine of the covenant, Hoeksema has shown that Scripture teaches a unilateral and unconditional covenant in which God enters into

friendship with His elect people in Jesus Christ. This was
a major breakthrough in the Reformed understanding of
God's covenant.

If one thing characterized Hoeksema's theology, it
was its God-centered character. To begin with God and
end with God — that was Hoeksema's purpose in all he
did.

Beginning with God in the doctrine of the covenant,
he demonstrated that God is in His own triune life a
covenant God who lives in blessed and perfect fellowship
with Himself. That covenant life which He eternally
enjoys, God chooses to reveal in His own eternal Son,
Jesus Christ, the Head of the covenant. He reveals it
through Christ by taking Christ, through the way of
Christ's cross, into the covenant life of the Trinity; and in
taking Christ into that covenant life, He takes all His elect
into the very life of the Trinity itself so that God and His
people may have joyful fellowship together for ever.

Such positive development of the truth is true church
reformation.

And such God-centered theology takes all glory from
man and gives it to God — where it belongs.

This is the history of the PRC.

This is important because precisely the doctrine of
God's covenant with His elect people was to be challenged in the Protestant Reformed Churches twenty-five
years after 1924.

It may appear to some to be somewhat strange that
controversy should once again erupt so soon after the
battles of 1924. How, some may ask, could the very
doctrines which were at the heart of the controversy when
the PRC began come under attack so soon after the
beginning of the denomination? Not even one generation
had passed and the same battle had to be fought anew.

It is probably not very easy to answer this question.
But several points must be made.

In the first place, not all who went along with the PRC at its beginning went for doctrinal reasons. This always happens in times of reformation. People may have various quarrels with their mother church, and these quarrels are not always over the truth of Scripture or the Reformed confessions. Many became a part of the PRC without being convinced of the truths for which the churches stood.

In close connection with this lies the more general truth that the church of Christ is constantly in need of reformation. Reformation, while being surely a mighty event at crucial times in the history of the church, is also an on-going calling of the people of God. Satan always seeks the overthrow of the church. And one way to destroy her is through false doctrine. The enemy is always there, within and without the walls of the church. Safety lies in constant vigilance.

The more immediate occasion for the controversy of 1953 lies in a church split in the Netherlands.

Earlier we spoke of two reformations which took place in the Netherlands in which the church of Christ was delivered from the apostate state church. The first was led by Hendrik DeCock; the second by Abraham Kuyper. The first took place in 1834. The second took place in 1886.

Because both were genuine church reformations, both also saw the necessity to join in the common cause of the Reformed faith in the Netherlands. A merger between them was accomplished in 1892 and resulted in the formation of the *Gereformeerde Kerken in Nederland* (the Reformed Churches in the Netherlands, the GKN).

But the union was not, in the long run, a successful one. Differences of doctrine remained between the two factions in the church; and these differences became a source of division. The division resulted in a split which took place in 1944 when the synod of the GKN, meeting in Sneek-Utrecht, deposed Dr. Klaas Schilder and other officebearers. This was the beginning of the Liberated Churches.

Close contact between the future leaders of the Liberated Churches and the PRC began as early as 1939, when Dr. Schilder visited this country and met with many PR ministers. The contact grew stronger in 1947, when once again Dr. Schilder visited this country, spent time in the homes of many PR ministers and officebearers, and lectured and preached in the churches.

These were the years after the war. Many people from the Reformed Churches in the Netherlands were seeking a new home in Canada or the United States. The people from the Liberated Churches were looking for a church home in this country and Canada and wondered whether the PRC would provide a congenial place for them.

This search of the Liberated for a church home proved to be an important one. If one doctrinal difference existed between Schilder and Hoeksema, and between Schilder's churches and the PRC, it was a difference on the doctrine of the covenant. Although already in 1939, during Schilder's first visit to this country, some hints of these differences came to the surface, in 1947 they became more widely known.

The differences were not of a minor sort. Schilder and the Liberated Churches held to a doctrine of the covenant which taught that the covenant between God and man was a pact or agreement between God and man; that, therefore, it is bilateral or two-sided, because an agreement cannot be made until two sides agree; that the covenant was established objectively with all the children of believers; and that the covenant was conditional, dependent upon faith. Only when man accepted the provisions of the covenant by faith would the covenant in its deepest spiritual sense be realized.

The PRC, under the leadership of Herman Hoeksema, held to a quite different idea. The covenant was, according to Hoeksema, a bond of friendship and fellowship between God and His people in Christ; it is established with the elect alone, i.e., with elect believers and their spiritual seed; it is solely and completely the work of God's grace, and is, therefore, unilateral or one-sided. God establishes His covenant with His people by taking them unconditionally into His own triune covenant life; and God maintains His covenant with His people by sovereign and unconditional grace even though they were and are often unfaithful. It is God's work and His work alone.

While the differences in viewpoint between the Liberated Churches and the Protestant Reformed Churches were over the doctrine of the covenant of grace, the issue itself, the deepest issue, was once again, as it had been in 1924, whether the grace of God is sovereign and particular. The Liberated denied this. They taught (and teach today) that the promise of the covenant is for all the baptized children and that the full realization of the covenant is dependent upon the fulfillment of the condition of faith. The promise is therefore a general and conditional promise and its fulfillment depends upon man's acceptance of it.

So, once more, the battle was joined.

And let there be no mistake about it, the question which the PRC faced was this: Are we to be faithful to our own heritage as Protestant Reformed Churches — or are we to compromise that heritage at a crucial point, the point of the truth of God's covenant? Are we to deny what we stood for in 1924 — or are we determined to be faithful to that doctrine? Were Hoeksema, Ophoff, and Danhof right in refusing to sign the Three Points — or were they being stubborn over insignificant differences of opinion? Was it right before God to form the Protestant Reformed Churches — or was it in actuality an act of schism in the body of Christ?

No one will deny that these are important questions.
They lie at the heart of the right of existence for the
Protestant Reformed Churches.

Apparently there were those who believed that 1924
was indeed a mistake and that the position on sovereign
and particular grace was wrong. Apparently there were
those who were willing to sacrifice the distinctive truth of
the covenant for the sake of growth.

The options were clear. If the PRC were willing to
adopt the Liberated view of the covenant, the hundreds or
thousands of immigrants streaming to this land would
have been more than willing to join the PRC; and the
mother church in the Netherlands would have been able
to establish close sister-church relations with the PRC.
But another possibility existed. The PRC, though aware
of the differences between itself and the Liberated on the
doctrine of the covenant, could have declared these differences non-confessional, and, therefore, not important.
Then the PRC ecclesiastical roof would have been wide
enough to shelter under it people holding diverse views.

It would have been a relatively simple matter. It could
have been done quite easily simply by taking the position, officially or unofficially, that the question of the
covenant was extra-confessional; i.e., not settled by the
confessions and therefore an open question in the PRC.
The churches would have grown dramatically and the
denomination would soon have more than doubled in
size.

Many in the PRC wanted that. Many ministers wanted
that. Also many officebearers and many influential leaders in the churches pleaded for that. The result was that
the covenant views of the Liberated began to be openly
defended within the churches on the pulpit, in the Catechism classes where the children and young people were
taught, in various publications, and in private conversa-
tions.

It was really in the church papers that the long and difficult battle began.

When some of the ministers in the PRC began to defend conditional theology, they made use of a church paper called *Concordia* to do this. The magazine had appeared already in 1944, but, ironically, in defiance of its name, which means "harmony," it sowed discord and division in the church by agitating for a conditional theology.

Because it entered nearly every home in the denomination, it sought to introduce this false doctrine in every home. And because Protestant Reformed homes were, above all, covenant homes, an open defense of a conditional covenant was a direct attack on the spiritual structure of the home.

Such an attack had to be answered. Rev. Herman Hoeksema, editor-in-chief of the *Standard Bearer,* began immediately to use the paper for a defense of the truth of a sovereign and unconditional salvation. For about five years the controversy waged unabated in the church papers.

But the battle for the truth of sovereign and particular grace as applied to the covenant was also attacked on another front. It was strange how it all happened, but it brought the issues to the broader assemblies.

Although Herman Hoeksema had developed his covenant views over the years, and although his development of these views was based solidly on the confessions of the PRC (the Heidelberg Catechism, the Confession of Faith, and the Canons of Dordt), no ecclesiastical assembly had ever made any statement concerning the doctrine of the covenant or its official status within the churches. For this reason, some thought the PRC did not have an official covenant view. And in a way that was correct.

When immigrants from the Netherlands, mostly from the Liberated Churches, wanted to know whether the

PRC had an official covenant view, and, if so, what it was, the question was not so easy to answer.

The Mission Committee, responsible for organizing immigrants into PR congregations if they so desired, came to the synod of the PRC in 1950 to ask for a statement on this question.

The synod of 1950, in response to this request, drew up a document which became known as the *Declaration of Principles* (see Appendix, p. 203). It was to be used on the mission field as a statement of what the PRC believed on the key question of sovereign and particular grace as applied to the well-meant offer of the gospel; the question whether grace was particular to the elect or common to all men; and the question of the conditionality or unconditionality of the covenant.

The *Declaration of Principles* was not intended to be and could not, by any stretch of the imagination, be construed to be another confession alongside the three forms of unity. Some charged that this was the case and that the PRC required loyalty to more than the three forms of unity, namely to a fourth confession which was drawn up by the PRC.

But this explanation was unjust and unwarranted. The document clearly showed that the entire heritage of Reformed confessions, both major and minor, taught a sovereignly particular and unconditional covenant.

The synod of 1950, with almost no dissenting votes, provisionally adopted the statement. It was provisionally adopted because it was sent back to the churches for examination and discussion with a view to final approval at the synod of 1951.

It seems that it was only after synod met that the defenders of a conditional theology realized what had happened. Less than two months after synod concluded its meetings the opposition began to be heard. The debate was in the church papers and in the consistory rooms to which the synod had sent the document for discussion.

The attacks against the *Declaration* were at two points. The first involved a church political question. The opponents of the *Declaration* argued that no synod might initiate such a document, but that a request for it had to come to synod via a consistory and a classis. This ignored the fact that the request had come from the Mission Committee, a committee of synod, appointed to carry out synod's mandates and charged with coming to synod with reports and requests relating to the mission work of the churches.

In close connection with this church political objection, it was argued, especially by the Liberated people, that the *Declaration* was really another confession, and that as a confession it made binding in the churches something which the confessions themselves did not require.

The synod, however, insisted that the *Declaration* was nothing more than quotations from the confessions proving that the truth of the unconditionality of salvation in general, and an unconditional covenant in particular, was precisely the position of those creeds to which the PRC were bound.

But the doctrinal objections were the fiercest. The *Declaration* emphatically proved that the great Reformation truths of sovereign and particular grace, as that grace was rooted in double predestination, makes God's covenant of grace His work, which He realizes without conditions, by taking His people alone into that covenant and preserving them in it until they reach glory. These great truths were anathema to those defending conditionality in the covenant. They did all in their power, therefore, to prevent the *Declaration* from being adopted.

Nevertheless, it was adopted by the synod of 1951, though by a margin of one vote. Following synods were bombarded with protests against the decision of 1951, but the protests were never treated because in the meantime the split had come.

Against the background of this raging controversy, dissension and schism arose in First Protestant Reformed Church. In a way, it was well that the differences in doctrine should come to a head in this congregation. It was, after all, the congregation of which Rev. Herman Hoeksema was pastor. It was the congregation which had been expelled from the Christian Reformed Church in 1924. As such it was the flagship of the denomination. It was far and away the largest congregation, numbering over 550 families. Because of its size it had three pastors: Rev. Herman Hoeksema, Rev. Cornelius Hanko, and Rev. Hubert DeWolf.

While Revs. Hoeksema and Hanko were deeply committed to the doctrines of sovereign grace, Rev. DeWolf was not. He was intent on promoting, along with many others, a conditional theology.

While he promoted his theology in catechism classes, societies, and personal contact, he finally brought it to the pulpit on April 15, 1951, when he made the bold statement in a sermon on the parable of the rich man and Lazarus: "God promises to every one of you that if you believe you will be saved."

Although he was referring more generally to the preaching of the gospel, he was, with that statement, clearly adopting the Liberated position. The promise in the preaching is for everyone who hears the gospel. Its realization in the heart is dependent upon the fulfillment of the condition of faith.

By making the preaching a statement of a general and conditional promise, DeWolf succeeded in showing clearly the connection between the Liberated view of a general and conditional promise in baptism and the CR heresy of a well-meant offer, conditioned by faith.

The statement brought protests from members of the

congregation and put the problem squarely in the hands of the elders. The consistory of First Church found it difficult to deal with the problem, chiefly because the elders reflected in their own ranks the divisions in the congregation.

The congregation was deeply affected. Discussions and debates were constantly carried on over the issues. Divisions and disagreements made the joy of the communion of saints difficult. Families and friends were driven apart. The worship of God on the Lord's Day was seriously affected by the lack of unity.

Because the consistory was unable to come to a resolution of the problem, the issues aggravated First Church for almost a year and a half, until they began to fade somewhat into the background, and the hope was even expressed that the whole difficulty could be resolved in such a way that the congregation would remain intact and the differences forgotten.

But then everything changed once more. On September 14, 1952, DeWolf threw caution to the winds and openly affirmed his commitment to conditional theology. It was a preparatory sermon, preached with a view to the administration of the Lord's Supper on the following Lord's Day. In the sermon, based on Matthew 18:3, DeWolf made the statement: "Our act of conversion is a prerequisite to enter the kingdom of heaven."

The congregation nearly exploded, and once again the elders had to take up the issues. No longer could differences be forgotten. Something had to be done, and done soon.

And so things began to move swiftly. In February of 1953, the elders subjected DeWolf to an examination of his orthodoxy, as the church order requires. Because the men who supported DeWolf were at this time in the majority in the consistory, his examination was approved and he was cleared of all heresy charges.

Some elders, however, not agreeing that the examination proved that DeWolf was orthodox, protested the decision of the consistory and appealed it to the next meeting of Classis East, in April of the same year.

And so the issue came to classis.

The classis, in dealing with the matter, made it its first order of business to appoint a committee of three ministers and two elders to study the whole case and to come to classis with advice. When the committee reported, it became obvious that the committee was split. The three ministers, in a very lengthy report to classis, made an attempt to give to DeWolf's statements an orthodox interpretation. The two elders did not. They prepared a one-page report in which they demonstrated that the statements were contrary to Scripture and the Reformed confessions and had to be condemned.

The report of the two elders was given a powerful boost by DeWolf's own repudiation of the majority report on the floor of the classis. The result was the adoption of the minority report of the two elders. The classis decided that these two statements were heretical and that DeWolf had to apologize publicly for them or be subject to the discipline of the church. It was furthermore decided that the elders who agreed with DeWolf's theology had to apologize for their heresy or be disciplined by the consistory.

A committee was appointed by classis to bring the decision to the consistory of First Church and to plead with DeWolf and the elders who supported him to confess their heresy and seek again the truth as it is in Christ.

This committee met with the consistory on June 1, 1953. By a majority vote of the elders the advice of classis was adopted by the consistory. Further action was postponed until June 15, on which night DeWolf was given an apology which the consistory expected him to make. However, instead of doing what the classis and the consistory required of him, he made another "apology," one which in no way admitted that his statements were heretical. Rather, he apologized for the lack of clarity in the statements and for the misunderstandings that arose because of this lack of clarity.

A meeting of the consistory on June 21 ended in chaos because the elders supporting DeWolf insisted on their right to vote — even though the consistory had already condemned their position at the meeting of June 1. On the next night, Revs. Hoeksema and Hanko met with the faithful elders from First Church and the consistory of Fourth Protestant Reformed Church (as the church order requires) and formally suspended DeWolf and deposed from office the elders who supported him.

Upon hearing of this, DeWolf's supporters immediately took over the church property, changed the locks, and barred anyone but their supporters from using the premises. The following Sunday the faithful people in First Church met and worshiped in the chapel of Grand Rapids Christian High School.

The end was not yet.

When Classis East met again in July of 1953, two sets of delegates, both claiming to represent First Church, were present: Rev. DeWolf and an elder, and Rev. Hanko and an elder. The classis decided, after hearing the history of what had transpired since its last meeting, that Rev. Hanko and his elder represented the First Protestant Reformed Church, while Rev. DeWolf and his elder did not.

When this decision had been taken, a number of ministers and elders, all supporters of DeWolf, rose from their seats and left the classis.

So the split that had begun in First Church now spread through the whole of Classis East.

It was not long before Classis West was also split. The matter of DeWolf's deposition had come to Classis West from several consistories. As the church order requires, First's consistory had notified all the churches of the suspension of DeWolf. This notification of DeWolf's suspension, for some strange reason, was brought to Classis West at its September meeting. It was strange because the material had no business at Classis West. The notifications of DeWolf's suspension were sent to all the consistories so that no other consistory would, inadvertently, open its pulpit to DeWolf. If those consistories which received the notification had objections to it, the course of action which they should have followed was the procedure of the church order: Protest to First Church itself, and, if necessary, carry the protest to Classis East and synod.

But Classis West chose to ignore the proper procedure. At its meeting, the actions of both First's consistory and Classis East were condemned without any opportunity for either body to explain and defend itself.

Although most ministers and the majority of the people in the West supported DeWolf, there were also faithful people in that part of the churches. The result was that the tremors of the split in the East rolled like shock waves through the West, and the chasm between the two groups in the East spread to the West.

The split was complete.

When the dust had settled it became obvious that the split had not only torn the denomination apart, but that it had resulted in the loss of a majority of members. The *Yearbook* of 1953 lists 24 churches, 29 ministers, 6063 individuals. The *Yearbook* of 1954 lists 16 churches, 14 ministers, 2353 members. A very small denomination had become still smaller.

Not only had the denomination been reduced in size, but friends and families had been separated, and the bitterness which all controversy engenders remained for years.

Worse yet, the work of the churches was made much more difficult. Mission work temporarily stopped. The seminary continued, though with a sharply reduced enrollment. The energy of the churches was devoted to the battles for the faith and the legal wrangles over property which followed the split. Much important work went undone. The Christian schools, supported by parents of the denomination, were hard hit and had a more difficult struggle to continue. A great battle-weariness settled over the people of God. Though victorious, the troops were wounded and bleeding.

It was a high price to pay to maintain the truth.

Undoubtedly the reaction of many to such a struggle was that the issues involved were simply not worth the high cost that had to be paid.

The CRC, to which DeWolf and all his followers returned before a decade had transpired, welcomed back those who left the PRC as a kind of justification of their discipline of Hoeksema, Ophoff, and Danhof in 1925.

Many throughout the church world could hardly understand why seemingly so much was made out of so little. And the general attitude was: Why carry issues of such inconsequence to the point that a church is split?

Even many in our own denomination wondered whether it was all worth the price that had to be paid.

It is indeed a question that has to be answered.

The heart of the question lies at this point: Were the issues that were debated and over which there was disagreement important?

The answer to that question has to be an unqualified Yes.

Several reasons can be mentioned why the issue was important, so important that if the result involved a church split, it had to be pressed nonetheless.

The first reason is without doubt the most important. The issue of an unconditional vs. a conditional covenant is an issue that involves one's doctrine of God. If God's covenant of grace is established with all children of believers, and if final and full participation in that covenant depends upon the fulfillment of conditions, then the realization of the covenant depends upon the free will of man.

Insofar as salvation, or the covenant of grace, depends upon the free will of man, it does not depend upon sovereign grace. Then God is not sovereign any longer in the work of salvation; man has some sovereignty of his own. But a denial of the sovereignty of God is a denial of God. God is either absolutely sovereign or He is not God at all. The truth of God Himself is at stake.

Secondly, the controversy was important because the issues were fundamentally no different from the great issues in which the church has been embroiled over the centuries. The truth of God's absolute sovereignty over against the free will of man was defended by Augustine in his battle with Pelagius, by Luther in his battle against Erasmus, by Calvin when he defended sovereign predestination against the attacks of Bolsec, by Dordt in its death struggle with the Arminians, and by DeCock and Kuyper when they led the faithful out of the apostate state church.

Thirdly, the issues were important because the right of the PRC to a separate existence was called into question. The PRC were born out of 1924 and the struggle in the CRC over the question of whether grace is common and resistible, or whether it is particular and sovereign. In holding to the latter, men of God were expelled from the CR communion. A new denomination was born.

The right of the PRC to exist separately as a denomination was challenged in the controversy of 1953. The doctrines in question were the same as they were in 1924. Is grace common and the reception of it dependent upon the will of man? Or is grace, also in the covenant, particular, i.e., only for the elect, and sovereign in its execution?

If those who agreed with DeWolf and eventually left the PRC, only in time to return to the CRC, were right in their conditional theology, then the entire PR denomination should have gone back, with an apology on its lips, to the CRC. There was need then to confess that Hoeksema, Ophoff, and Danhof had been wrong and had committed the terrible sin of schism in the body of Christ.

But De Wolf and those with him were wrong. The PRC did nothing else but stand for what was always their position and for what had been the position of the church of Christ through the ages.

God has blessed that decision. The PRC remain, under God's blessing, a strong witness of the truth of sovereign grace.

Section II

A Catechism on the Doctrinal Issues of 1924

Herman Hoeksema

On the Arminian Doctrine of Common Grace

1. Why are you a member of the Protestant Reformed Churches?

Because it is my conviction that everyone is conscience-bound to join himself to the purest manifestation of the church of God on earth.

2. How do you determine what is the purest manifestation of the church in the world?

By the criterion of the distinguishing marks of the true church.

3. Which are these distinguishing marks of the true church?

The pure preaching of the Word of God; the administration of the sacraments according to the institution of Christ; and the proper exercise of Christian discipline.

4. Is it a great sin to unite oneself with a church other than that which is, according to one's conviction, the purest manifestation of the true church?

It is; for, by doing so one knowingly cooperates with those forces that always tend to the development of the false church. A church need not be wholly false and

corrupt to justify separation from its fellowship. Every
church is false in the measure that it departs from the
Word of God, corrupts the sacraments, and becomes lax
or perverse in the exercise of Christian discipline.

**5. But why cannot you be a member of the Christian
Reformed Church of America?**
Because they would demand of me to express conformity with the Three Points adopted in 1924. These points
were added to the confession of the Reformed churches
by the Synod of Kalamazoo in 1924, and since that time
they are an integral part of the confession of the Christian
Reformed Church. And they officially expel or bar from
their fellowship every one that will subscribe to the three
forms of unity, viz., the Heidelberg Catechism, the Belgic
or Netherlands Confession, and the Canons of Dordrecht,
but refuses to express agreement with the Three Points.
And seeing that I cannot sign these points of doctrine they
certainly make it impossible for me to affiliate myself
with them.

**6. Which are those Three Points of which you are speak-
ing?**
a.   "Relative to the first point which concerns the
favorable attitude of God towards humanity in general and not only towards the elect, synod declares it
to be established according to Scripture and the Confessions that, apart from the saving grace of God
shown only to those that are elect unto eternal life,
there is also a certain favor or grace of God which He
shows to His creatures in general. This is evident
from the scriptural passages quoted and from the
Canons of Dordrecht, II, 5 and III/IV, 8 and 9, which
deal with the general offer of the gospel, while it also
appears from the citations made from Reformed writers of the most flourishing period of Reformed theol-

ogy that our Reformed writers from the past favored this view."

b. "Relative to the second point, which is concerned with the restraint of sin in the life of the individual man and in the community, the synod declares that there is such a restraint of sin according to Scripture and the Confessions. This is evident from the citations from Scripture and from the Netherlands Confession, Arts. 13 and 36, which teach that God by the general operations of His Spirit, without renewing the heart of man, restrains the unimpeded breaking out of sin, by which human life in society remains possible; while it is also evident from the quotations from Reformed writers of the most flourishing period of Reformed theology, that from ancient times our Reformed fathers were of the same opinion."

c. "Relative to the third point, which is concerned with the question of civil righteousness as performed by the unregenerate, synod declares that according to Scripture and the Confessions the unregenerate, though incapable of doing any saving good, can do civil good. This is evident from the quotations from Scripture and from the Canons of Dordrecht, III/IV, 4, and from the Netherlands Confession, Article 36, which teach that God without renewing the heart so influences man that he is able to perform civil good; while it also appears from the citations from Reformed writers of the most flourishing period of Reformed theology, that our Reformed fathers from ancient times were of the same opinion."

7. *But why can you not subscribe to them?*
Because they embody the doctrine of common grace, which is contrary to Scripture and to the Reformed standards.

8. What is this doctrine of common grace which you consider unscriptural and un-Reformed?

To answer this question adequately it will be expedient that I explain, first, the doctrine as it was introduced and expounded by Arminius and his followers in the beginning of the seventeenth century; secondly, the doctrine as it was most elaborately developed by Dr. Abraham Kuyper; and thirdly, the same doctrine as it is embodied in the Three Points, for these points really represent a combination of the Arminian and Kuyperian view of common grace.

9. Who was Arminius?

James Arminius (Jakobus Harmsen) was a Dutch theologian of the Reformed Churches of the Netherlands. He was born in Oudewater, the Netherlands, in 1560, one year after Guido de Brés composed his Articles of Faith, now our Belgic Confession, three years before the Heidelberg Catechism was published, and four years before the great Reformer of Geneva finished his life's work. He studied at the University of Leyden, from which he graduated in 1582; continued his studies under Beza at Geneva, where that disciple of Calvin was at that time lecturing on the epistle to the Romans; made a visit to Padua and Rome; returned to the Netherlands in 1587, and became minister of the divine Word in the Reformed Church of Amsterdam. Although even during his ministry he created suspicion with respect to his orthodoxy, and although he found strong opposition especially on the part of Gomarus, who at that time was professor of theology in Leyden, Arminius was appointed professor in the University of Leyden and became co-laborer with Gomarus till the day of his death on October 19, 1609.

10. What influence did Arminius have as professor in Leyden?

It soon became evident that in his views of predestination he departed from the accepted Reformed faith. He
not only developed these deviating views but instilled
them into the minds and hearts of his students, not only
in the lecture room but also in private sessions with his
disciples. And being an able scholar and of a pleasing and
refined personality, his influence was profound and wide-
spread, as soon became evident in the preaching from
many a Reformed pulpit in the Netherlands.

11. Which views did Arminius personally develop?
The following:

a. That God ordained Jesus Christ to be Mediator.
This proposition, though it might be criticized for its
vagueness and indefiniteness, could of course be sub-
scribed to by all that embraced the Reformed faith. In
its general form it could not be attacked, and it carefully avoided the questions that occupied the minds of
many in the Reformed Churches of the Netherlands at
that time.

b. That God determined to accept in Christ all peni-
tent and believing sinners, and to condemn all that
remained impenitent and unbelieving under the
preaching of the gospel. Even this proposition, as it
stands, could not very well be gainsaid. However, it
very readily implied a serious departure from the
Reformed faith. For, if Arminius had been asked to
explain this second proposition, it would have become evident that in his opinion it depended, not on
God's sovereign determination, but on the free will of
man whether or not he would repent and believe in
Christ.

c. That God ordained the means of grace unto salvation. Again, on the face of it, this statement is so
evidently true that no one would think of rejecting it.

Yet, in the mind of Arminius it implied that God on His part earnestly willed and revealed the salvation of all that hear the gospel and that He provided all equally with the means of grace. These means of grace, therefore, constituted a general and well-meaning offer of salvation to all that hear the Word preached.

d. That God, foreknowing who would believe and repent and who would not believe in Christ, foreordained particular persons unto salvation. This last proposition rather clearly expresses Arminius' conception of predestination. He apparently did not deny the doctrine of election and reprobation. Yet, by stating that God's election and rejection depended upon His foreknowledge, he actually made God's decree dependent on the will of man. This is the Arminian doctrine of election and reprobation on the basis of foreseen faith and foreseen unbelief.

12. Did the death of Arminius in 1609 check the progress of his deviant views?

On the contrary, the doctrine of Arminius was after the heart of man, and he had gained many disciples. The Arminian views were preached from many a pulpit and taught in many a school. The followers of Arminius also further developed and more clearly expounded the views of their master. As early as 1610 they were able to offer five propositions as an expression of their beliefs. These were called the Remonstrance.

13. Which is the first proposition of this Remonstrance?

"That God by an eternal, unchangeable purpose in Christ Jesus, His Son, hath determined out of the fallen, sinful race of men, to save in Christ, for Christ's sake and through Christ, those, who, through the grace of the Holy Spirit shall believe in this His Son, Jesus, and shall persevere in this faith and obedience of faith, through this grace, even unto the end; and on the other hand to leave the incorrigible and unbelieving in sin and under wrath and to condemn them as alienate from Christ; according to the word of the gospel in John 3:36: He that believeth on the Son hath everlasting life, but he that obeyeth not the Son shall not see life, the wrath of God abideth on him; and according to other passages of Scripture also."

14. Could there be any objection to the doctrine expressed in this proposition?

Seemingly not. The superficial reader might easily accept this as sound Reformed truth. No doubt the terminology of this proposition is calculated to deceive the minds of the imprudent and inexperienced just like the terminology of many a modern sermon and also of the Three Points. It seems to teach an eternal and unchangeable counsel of God, and apparently it ascribes all the work of faith and salvation to the grace of the Holy Spirit.

15. Do you mean to say, then, that in this first proposition the Remonstrants deny the Reformed doctrine of predestination?

I most certainly maintain this.

16. But how can you sustain this position?

By pointing out that in this first proposition the Arminians, or Remonstrants, do not teach that God's counsel is sovereign and independent, but contingent and dependent on the faith and unbelief of man. The objects of God's election are *those that believe;* the objects of reprobation are the *incorrigible and unbelieving.* This is identical with the last proposition of Arminius, that God's election and reprobation are determined by His foreknowledge of those who would and those who would not believe in Christ.

17. How would you express the difference between this proposition and the Reformed faith sharply?

Thus: according to the first proposition of the Remonstrance, the counsel of God is determined by the faith and unbelief of man; according to the Reformed view, the counsel of God is the ultimate determining cause of faith and unbelief both.

18. Did you say: also of unbelief?

Most certainly; God did not only determine who should, but also who should not believe in Christ. And in both elements of this determination He is absolutely sovereign.

19. But do not the Arminians clearly state that a man can believe through the grace of God only?

They do, I admit. But this does not alter the tendency of their first proposition in the least. For they would explain that God chose those *who should be willing* to receive the grace of the Holy Spirit, and that He rejected those *who should not be so willing,* which clearly makes the will of man the determining cause of the counsel of God.

20. But is this such a serious difference that it would justify separation from a church that holds the Arminian view?

It most certainly is. For, the deepest question underlying this difference, and determined by it, is whether God or man is really *God.*

21. How does the second proposition of the Remonstrance read?

"That agreeably thereto Jesus Christ, the Saviour of the world, died for all men and for every man, so that He has obtained for them all, by His death on the cross, redemption and the forgiveness of sins; yet so, that no one actually enjoys this forgiveness of sins except the believer, according to the word of the gospel in John 3:16: For God so loved the world that He gave His only begotten Son, that whosoever believeth on Him should not perish but have everlasting life; and in the first epistle of John 2:2: And he is the propitiation for our sins and not for ours only, but for the sins of the whole world."

22. What is your objection to this article of the Remonstrance?

That it teaches the error of universal atonement, maintaining that Jesus Christ died for all and every man.

23. But does not the article plainly restrict the actual fruit of the death of Christ to believers?

It does; yet, while it also maintains that in Christ's and God's intention the suffering of the cross is for all and every man, it makes the cross of Christ of none effect for many. And again, the determining cause of the effect or non-effect of the death of Christ is the will of man.

24. Is this also a serious error?

Most certainly; for it necessarily implies the denial of the truth of vicarious atonement. Either Christ's death is atoning so that it actually is the satisfaction of God's justice for all our sins (but then all for whom He died and rose are certainly justified and saved); or, by the death of Christ all for whom He died are not certainly justified and saved (but then His death cannot have been atoning). The doctrine that Christ died for all men is the beginning of Modernism.

25. What is the third proposition of the Remonstrance?

"That man has not saving grace of himself, nor of the energy of his free will, as he, in the state of his apostasy and sin, can of and by himself neither think, will, nor do

anything that is truly good (such as saving faith emi-
nently is); but that it is needful that he be born again of
God in Christ, through His Holy Spirit, and renewed in
understanding, inclination or will, and all his powers in
order that he may rightly understand, think, will, and
effect what is truly good, according to the word of Christ
in John 15:5: Apart from me ye can do nothing."

26. Is there any objectionable element in this third article?

Not when it is considered all by itself. The truth of the
total depravity of the natural man and of his total incapa-
bility of contributing anything to his own salvation is
certainly expressed in the strongest terms. Yet, this
article and its strong language are deceptive, as is evident
as soon as it is read in the light of the preceding propositions and of the article that immediately follows. For,
although the Remonstrants seem to teach that salvation
must be solely the work of God and that the natural man
without grace can do nothing that is truly good, yet they
in fact deny this when they presently add that man must
show himself worthy to receive this grace. The grace of
God is not irresistible.

27. Where do they teach this error?

In the fourth proposition of the Remonstrance, which
reads as follows:

"That the grace of God is the beginning, continuance,
and accomplishment of all good, even to this extent that
the regenerate man himself without prevenient, assisting, awakening, following, and cooperative grace, can
neither think, will, nor do good, nor withstand any temptations to evil; so that all good deeds and movements that
can be conceived must be ascribed to the grace of God in
Christ. But as respects the mode of the operation of this
grace, it is not irresistible, inasmuch as it is written

concerning many that they have resisted the Holy Ghost
— Acts 7 and elsewhere in many places."

28. What is the serious error of this proposition?

That it reduces the grace of God and the work of the
Holy Spirit to a mere offer and an attempt to persuade the
sinner to accept the offer. It is a denial of the efficacious
character of the grace of God.

29. Does the article not imply a contradiction?

It does; for, on the one hand, it asseverates that the
grace of God is the very beginning of all good; and, on the
other hand, it leaves the natural man the power to will or
not to will, to resist or not to resist this grace of the Holy
Spirit. But surely, to will the grace of God is very positively a good. If the grace of God is really the beginning
of all good man can do, it cannot follow but must needs
precede the will to receive it.

30. What, then, is this article in effect?

A denial of the doctrine of total depravity. For if man
is really totally depraved by nature, so that he is wholly
incapable of doing, thinking, or willing any good thing; if
it is maintained that he is carnal and sold under sin, and
that his mind is enmity against God, he surely cannot long
for or will to receive the grace of God.

31. Is there any relation between the denial of the sover-eign character of God's decree of predestination and the denial of the total depravity of the sinner?

There is. The one demands the other. He that denies
the doctrine of sovereign election and reprobation must
also deny the total depravity of the natural man. If
salvation is an offer, there must be left in the sinner to
whom the offer is made the power to accept the offer. For,

to offer any good thing to one who we know cannot accept
it is mere mockery.

32. What is the last article of the Remonstrance?

"That those who are incorporated into Christ by a true
faith, and have thereby become partakers of His life-
giving Spirit, have thereby full power to strive against
Satan, sin, the world, and their own flesh, and to win the
victory, it being well understood that it is ever through
the assisting grace of the Holy Ghost; and that Jesus
Christ assists them through His Spirit in all temptations,
extends to them His hand; and if only they are ready for
the conflict and desire His help, and are not inactive,
keeps them from falling, so that they by no craft or power
of Satan can be misled, nor plucked out of Christ's hand,
according to the word of Christ, John 10:28: No one can
pluck them out of my hand. But whether they are capable
through negligence or forsaking again the first beginning
of their life in Christ, of again returning to this present
evil world, of turning away from the holy doctrine which
was delivered them, of losing a good conscience, of be-
coming devoid of grace, that must be more particularly
determined out of the Holy Scriptures, before we ourselves can teach it with full persuasion of our minds."

33. What is objectionable in this last article?

That it constitutes a denial of the perseverance of the
saints, even unto the end, through the almighty grace of
the Holy Spirit.

34. But do not the Remonstrants leave the doctrine of the perseverance of saints an open question?

In the last part of the article they appear to leave this
matter open for debate, for they state that they are not
fully persuaded in their own minds whether the saints
can fall away from grace. But in the first part of this

proposition they clearly deny the certainty of the perseverance of believers.

35. How do they do this?

By saying that Christ will assist them through His Spirit and keep them from falling, *if only they are ready for the conflict and desire His help and are not inactive.* For in this statement the grace of Christ whereby only the saints are able to persevere is made dependent once more upon the will and desire and work of man. And the truth is that their very readiness for the conflict and desire to receive the help of Christ is dependent upon the grace of God, which is always first.

36. What synod marks the close of the Arminian controversy in the Netherlands?

The famous Synod of Dordrecht of 1618-1619.

37. What was done by this synod?

In five canons or chapters of doctrine the synod developed and set forth the true doctrine of Scripture, as confessed by the Reformed churches, and rejected the errors of the Remonstrants, always stating the grounds on which these errors are rejected. These Canons of Dordrecht constitute a part of the Reformed confessions. They are printed in the back of every *Psalter* in use by our churches and should be studied by every member of the Protestant Reformed Churches.

38. What may be learned from the five articles of the Remonstrants?

That one may express himself in rather strong terms as believing in the Reformed truth, while in actual fact he denies the very fundamental principles of the Reformed doctrine and confessions.

39. What else may be learned from these articles?

That there is an inseparable connection between one's view of God and his conception of man. The whole-hearted confession of the sovereignty of God is content to leave man as he is by nature, apart from the grace of God, dead in sin and misery. But in the same measure as the sovereign grace of God is denied, man must be represented as having the power to do good.

40. Of what significance is this with respect to the Three Points of 1924?

It is a striking fact that, like the Remonstrance of the Arminians, they also declare themselves concerning man and God. And, while speaking of a certain common or general grace of God in the first point, they attribute the power to do good to the natural, unregenerated man in the second and third. But of this we must speak later.

On the Kuyperian View
of Common Grace

1. What was the development with respect to the Reformed doctrine after the Synod of Dordrecht?

There was very little progress in the development of the doctrine of sin and grace according to the Reformed conception. The eighteenth century presents a most miserable picture. Rationalism lifted up its head and claimed to possess the sole right of supremacy in the realm of theology. Whatever was not logically and rationally comprehensible it dismissed as unknowable; it laughed the miraculous out of court and God out of the universe; it denied the possibility of revelation and of the Bible as the Word of God; Christ was degraded into mere man; and the faith of the church was declared to be vain.

2. What was the attitude of the church over against this rationalistic spirit?

She assumed an apologetic position. Tempted to meet the enemy on his own basis, she desperately attempted to hold fast that which she had, to defend the truth rationally, not understanding that by this method she denied herself, only to see the very treasures of the truth she tried to save slip out of her hand. Men who meant well fought badly, awkwardly employing the weapons of the enemy. Bulwark after bulwark they surrendered, until they themselves paid homage to the goddess of reason and acknowledged her supremacy in the domain where properly faith should rule.

3.   What was the result for the church?

Gradually the most fundamental truths were denied, and false doctrines crept into the church. The divinity of Christ, His resurrection, His vicarious atonement, not to speak of such fundamentals as predestination and total depravity, were not considered essential anymore as elements in any basis of unity. By many Christ was considered the ideal man; salvation was to be delivered from a set of wrong notions; sanctification was to be delivered from some bad habits; the truth was lost; the church was dead; rationalism had gained its victory.

4.   Was this, generally speaking, the condition in the Reformed Churches of the Netherlands?

It was; and especially after 1816 the confessions were no longer maintained; the clergy were at liberty to teach as they pleased.

5.   What happened in 1834?

This was the year of the Separation under the leadership of Hendrik DeCock, and a new day dawned for the Reformed faith in the insignificant village of Ulrum, Groningen.

6.   What was the principle of the Separation?

It was a return to the faith of the fathers, especially with respect to the doctrine of sin and grace. Once more it was emphasized that with respect to the work of salvation God is all and man is nothing, that salvation is of the Lord, and that He is merciful to whom He wills. Yet there was no further and richer development of the Reformed faith by the leaders of the Separation. They returned to the principles of the Synod of Dordrecht.

7. Was there no other separation from the state church of the Netherlands after 1834?

There was in 1886 a secession from the established church called the Doleantie. The main leader of this movement was Dr. Abraham Kuyper.

8. What became of the churches of the Separation of 1834 and of the Doleantie of 1886?

They united into one denomination in 1892 and are now known as the *Gereformeerde Kerken* of the Netherlands. A small group refusing to go along in this union and continuing a separate existence is known as the *Christelijke Gereformeerde Kerk.*

9. What is the significance of Dr. Kuyper in connection with our history?

He made an elaborate attempt to reconcile a certain theory of common grace with the Reformed conception of particular grace. Systematically he tried to develop his theory of common grace in the three volumes of what is usually considered his monumental work, *De Gemeene Gratie.*

10. Can you give a brief sketch of Dr. Kuyper's life and work?

Dr. Kuyper was born at Maassluis, October 29, 1837. His father was a minister in the Established Church. Young Abraham received his primary education in the public schools of Maassluis and Middleburg. His second- ary education he commenced at the Gymnasium (high school) of Middleburg, from which he graduated in 1855. He then followed the theological course at the University of Leyden, and there he received a thoroughly modern and liberal education. Having finished his course he became minister of the church at Beesd, where he came into contact with simple folk who adhered to the Reformed faith and by whom he was induced for the first time to consider the Reformed truth seriously. From 1867 to 1869 he served the Church of Utrecht, and there he began his fight for the liberation of the church from the bondage of the state. There also he came into frequent conflict with moderns, ethicals, and irenicals. In 1869 he accepted a call to Amsterdam, where he continued the battle for what he termed a Reformed, democratic, free, and independent church. He became editor of a paper, *De Standaard,* in 1872 and member of the Second Chamber of Parliament in 1874. Chiefly through his efforts the Free University of Amsterdam was established in 1880, where he became Professor of Theology. As has already been stated, it was chiefly by his genius that the movement of the Doleantie was inspired and sustained. In his later years he took a very active part in politics and was Prime Minister of the Netherlands in 1901 to 1905. He died November 8, 1920.

11. How ought we to estimate the life and work of Dr. Kuyper?

He was undoubtedly a man of keen intellect and mighty vision. He was possessed of an almost unbelievable capacity for work. He was a man of dominating character and strong willpower. He labored for the liberation of the church and for the revival of the Reformed faith and Calvinistic principles as he understood them, and he pursued the ideal of realizing these principles in every sphere of life. It cannot be denied, however, that his early training and liberal education left an impression upon him which he never entirely overcame. In his attempt to apply the principles of the Reformed faith to every sphere of life, he did not keep in view that the struggle of the people of God is a purely spiritual one. For the Reformed element in the Netherlands he desired and sought a place of power in the world, and in this pursuit of power the principles of the Word of God were not always maintained and applied. And it is in this light that we also must view the attempt to develop the theory of common grace alongside of the truth that the grace of God is particular. The theory served to create a synthesis between the church and the world.

12. What is the denotation of the word "grace" in the term "common grace" as used by Kuyper?

Kuyper makes a distinction between "common" and "special" grace. The latter only is of saving power and efficacy and is particular, that is, for the elect only; its fruit is eternal life and glory in Christ. The former is not saving but pertains only to the present life and history of man in the world and is universal or common to all men. To denote the distinction, Kuyper preferred to employ the word *gratie* to indicate common grace, while he used the term *genade* to denote special or particular grace. The fact remains, however, that also in the term "common grace" the word "grace" denotes an attitude and operation of lovingkindness or favor.

13. What may be considered Kuyper's chief purpose in developing the theory of common grace?

He sought to show that there still is good in the world and in the development of the human race in connection with all created things, and by the theory of common grace he offered an explanation of the good in the world in connection with the fall and the curse of God in the world and the total depravity of the natural man.

14. From what presupposition does Kuyper proceed in developing this view?

He maintains that if "common grace" had not intervened and begun to operate immediately after the fall, the end of all things would have been reached in Paradise with man's eating of the forbidden fruit; the whole world would have relapsed into a chaotic state; Adam would have died the complete and eternal death; and there would have been no history, no development of the human race in the world. As a result, there would have been no room for the establishment and development of God's covenant of grace in Christ, the elect would not have been born, Christ would not have come, and the works of God would have been completely spoiled and destroyed by the wiles of Satan. The latter's purpose would have been reached.

However, by His common grace God intervened, the universe did not suffer destruction, man did not immediately die, and the original divine idea and ordinance of creation can be and is realized in the history of this world. At the same time, a sphere is created for the realization and development of special grace in Christ Jesus.

He therefore conceives of the work of God in a dualistic way. God has an original purpose with creation, the normal development of all things under man as their king. This purpose is apparently frustrated by the temptation of the devil and sin. But through the operation of common grace God carries out the original idea and brings about a positively good development of the human race in connection with the earthly creation. But, on the other hand, God also carries out His purpose of predestination in the redemption of the elect and the damnation of the reprobate.

15. But does not Kuyper confuse the operation and effect of God's providence with that of His grace?

In as far as He ascribes the preservation and development of created things after the fall to God's common grace, he certainly calls grace what is merely God's providential care and government.

16. But is, then, the controversy about common grace not a mere quarrel about words?

No, for, first, it is by no means a harmless theory that confuses God's providence with His grace; and, secondly, the Kuyperian theory of common grace includes much more than this.

17. What else does it teach?

It does not merely teach that by the power of common grace the world is essentially sustained after the fall and the development of the human race made possible and assured, but also that good on the part of the fallen human race, in connection with all created things, has thus been guaranteed. In all progress and civilization, in science and art, in industry and commerce as carried on by the "world," in all the mighty works of the natural man, Kuyper perceives a positively good element. The natural man accomplishes, in actual fact, many good things and performs many good works. And that he is able to do this is to be attributed to the operation of God's common grace.

18. Does Kuyper, then, not profess to believe in the total depravity of the natural man?

He does. On the one hand he attempts to maintain that the natural man is wholly corrupt and incapable of doing any good; on the other hand, by the wonder of the common grace of God, which does not change the corruption of man's heart, He makes him perform many good works. The corrupt tree in Kuyper's conception bears good fruit.

19. But how does Kuyper try to explain this apparent contradiction?

First of all by the theory that common grace acts as a checking or restraining power:

a. Upon the curse of God in the universe, so that the world did not become chaos or hell.

b. Upon the physical existence of man, so that he did not immediately die the physical death.

c. Upon the ethical and moral corruption of man, so that he did not immediately become wholly corrupt in all his ways.

20. Does Kuyper, then, hold that man immediately after the fall did not really die?

Indeed, he does. The threat of God: "The day that thou eatest thereof thou shalt surely die," Kuyper explains not as a threat which God Himself would execute in His judgment, but as a fair warning that the result of eating of the forbidden fruit would be death, just as the result of touching an electric wire of heavy voltage must result in death, or as death is the inevitable result of taking poison. However, when man ate nevertheless, God spread the wings of His lovingkindness over him, intervened with the operation of His common grace, which then acted as an antidote against the spiritual poison man had taken. The result was:

a. That he did not immediately die the physical death, which certainly would have been the result, according to Kuyper, but for the intervention of common grace.

b. That he did not at once die the eternal death, which also would have followed immediately had it not been for the operation of common grace.

c. That he died the spiritual death only in principle. Also this death he did not die completely. The moral, spiritual-ethical corruption was complete only in principle, not in degree.

21. But how can mere restraint of corruption and death be productive of positive good?

This would, of course, be impossible. Hence, Kuyper also teaches that there is a constant operation of the common grace of God upon the mind and will of the natural man, whereby man is not regenerated, but yet so improved, even in his mind and will, that he is able to bring forth good works in the sphere of this present life.

22. But is, then, Kuyper's natural man in reality totally depraved?

Kuyper claims that he is, though in reality he is not. It is very evident that Kuyper's theory implies the concession that fallen man would have been totally corrupt if common grace had not checked corruption and improved upon him. Kuyper's natural man is:

a. A man who is unable to bring forth those good works that follow from the principle of regeneration, such as faith, hope, love, etc.

b. But a man, nevertheless, in whom a remnant of the original life and righteousness is left, so that he is able to live a good life in and for this world.

23. To what does Kuyper point as the basis for this operation of common grace?

To the covenant God established with Noah after the flood. This covenant, according to Kuyper, is not to be regarded as the covenant of grace in Christ, but as a covenant of universal friendship with the entire and fallen human race as such. Its blessings are temporal, are only for the present life, and are intended for the entire human race. In and through this covenant the natural and totally depraved man becomes God's friend and ally over against the devil and fights on God's side for the maintenance and development of a positively good life in the world.

24. Which are the three chief elements in the Kuyperian conception of common grace?

a. That, though with a view to eternity and the eternal blessedness of the kingdom, God is gracious only to the elect, with a view to things earthly and temporal, He is gracious to all men.

b. That, ever since the fall of man, there is a restraining influence of the common grace of God upon the physical and ethical corruption of the world and of the heart of man, so that the principle of total depravity cannot work through.

c. That there is a positive influence of God's common grace upon the mind and will of man, whereby he is so improved that he can still live a positively good life in the world.

25. What is the practical danger of this conception?

That it easily leads to the Arminian conception of common grace and to the Pelagian conception of the natural man, and that it serves as a bond of fellowship in this world between the children of light and the children of darkness. The antithesis is obliterated.

26. Is, then, this theory of common grace contrary to Scripture and the Reformed confessions?

It most certainly is.

27. Can you prove this?

Yes; but this we can more conveniently and in detail accomplish when we discuss the Three Points of 1924, as they were adopted by the synod of the Christian Reformed Church, for these are really an embodiment of the Kuyperian conception of common grace together with a mixture of Arminian common grace, especially in the first point.

28. But can you not point out some of the errors in Kuyper's conception and reasoning?

Certainly. He first of all errs when he states that the whole world would have become chaos and that man would have sunk into eternal death and hell immediately had it not been for the operation of common grace. For he fails to consider the fact that the world stood at the beginning of an organic development, that Adam stood at the head and was the first father and root of the entire human race, that as such he had sinned, and that the consummation of all things could not possibly have come in the beginning. Hell and destruction could not come till all that are lost in Adam are born and have filled the measure of iniquity.

29. What other error is implied in Kuyper's conception?

He confuses the moral and ethical with the purely physical. Sin could not possibly destroy all things essentially, though it change the ethical relation of man to God. Essentially things had not changed in the universe; neither had man's relation to created things when Adam sinned. Man after the fall was still king of the earthly creation, all things still serve him, and he was still called with all things to serve his God. This organic relation of all things, with the heart of man as its center, God maintained, not as Kuyper thinks by common grace, but merely by His providence. And thus maintaining the organic relation of all things with man as the center and head of the earthly creation, God also maintained His will concerning this organic whole, namely, that in and through man all things should serve Him and be subservient to His purpose, the glory of His name.

But the natural man, who is wholly incapable of doing any good, whose carnal mind is enmity against God, while he is maintained by God's providence in that position and calling, both with relation to all created things on the one hand and to God on the other, cannot, will not, and cannot will to do the will of God. He is still prophet, priest, and king, but of the devil and in covenant with him.   And while God in His providence and by the Word of His power sustains his nature as man, and sustains his relation to the universe, thus providing him with means to develop and realize his life in the organism of all things, with these things man is always the sinner, the ungodly, the object of the wrath of God, gathering for himself treasures of wrath in the day of final judgment.

However, there is an immediate operation of grace in Christ after the fall, whereby the covenant with the devil is broken and enmity is put between the seed of the serpent and the seed of the woman. This grace in Christ, however, whereby man becomes of the party of the living God over against Satan and all the powers of darkness, is realized along the line of election. Thus it happens that the elect and the reprobate, the righteous and the unrighteous, the godly and the ungodly have all things in common except grace. They are, for this present time, members of the same organism of the human race essentially; they live in the same organism of created things. But from an ethical-spiritual point of view they live from totally different principles.   And in the end God will realize His eternal kingdom and covenant in Christ, who is heir of all things, and in whom all things will forever serve man, that man may serve his God!

The Common Grace Theory
of the First Point

1. What do you mean by the "first point"?

The first of the three doctrinal declarations adopted by and added to the confessions of the Christian Reformed Church by the synod of those churches in 1924.

2. Can you quote it?

Yes; it reads as follows: "Relative to the first point which concerns the favorable attitude of God towards humanity in general and not only towards the elect, synod declares it to be established according to Scripture and the Confession that, apart from the saving grace of God shown only to those that are elect unto eternal life, there is also a certain favor or grace of God which He shows to His creatures in general. This is evident from the scriptural passages quoted and from the Canons of Dordrecht, II, 5 and III/IV, 8 and 9, which deal with the general offer of the gospel, while it also appears from the citations made from Reformed writers of the most flourishing period of Reformed theology that our Reformed writers from the past favored this view."

3. Which are the passages from the confessions mentioned in this first point?

They are the following:

Canons II, 5: "Moreover, the promise of the gospel is that whosoever believeth in Christ crucified, shall not

perish but have everlasting life. This promise, together
with the command to repent and believe, ought to be
declared and published to all nations, and to all persons
promiscuously and without distinction, to whom God out
of his good pleasure sends the gospel."

Canons III/IV, 8: "As many as are called by the
gospel, are unfeignedly called. For God hath most earnestly and truly shown in his Word, what is pleasing to
him, namely, that those who are called should come to
him. He, moreover, seriously promises eternal life and
rest to as many as shall come to him, and believe on him."

Canons III/IV, 9: "It is not the fault of the gospel, nor
of Christ, offered therein, nor of God, who calls men by
the gospel, and confers upon them various gifts, that
those who are called by the ministry of the word, refuse to
come and be converted...."

Thus far synod quoted the last article, which continues as follows:

"The fault lies in themselves; some of whom when
called, regardless of their danger, reject the word of life;
others, though they receive it, suffer it not to make a
lasting impression on their heart; therefore, their joy,
arising only from a temporary faith, soon vanishes, and
they fall away; while others choke the seed of the Word by
perplexing cares, and the pleasures of this world, and
produce no fruit. This our Saviour teaches in the parable
of the sower, Matthew 13."

**4. And which are the scriptural references adduced in
support of the first point?**

They are the following:

Psalm 145:9: "The LORD is good to all: and his tender
mercies are over all his works."

Matthew 5:44, 45: "But I say unto you, Love your
enemies, bless them that curse you, do good to them that
hate you, and pray for them which despitefully use you,

and persecute you; That ye may be the children of your Father which is in heaven: for he maketh his sun to rise on the evil and on the good, and sendeth rain on the just and on the unjust."

Luke 6:35, 36: "But love ye your enemies, and do good, and lend, hoping for nothing again; and your reward shall be great, and ye shall be the children of the Highest: for he is kind unto the unthankful and to the evil. Be ye therefore merciful, as your Father also is merciful."

Acts 14:16, 17: "Who in times past suffered all nations to walk in their own ways. Nevertheless he left not himself without witness, in that he did good, and gave us rain from heaven, and fruitful seasons, filling our hearts with food and gladness."

I Timothy 4:10: "For therefore we both labour and suffer reproach, because we trust in the living God, who is the Saviour of all men, specially of those that believe."

Romans 2:4: "Or despisest thou the riches of his goodness and forbearance and longsuffering; not knowing that the goodness of God leadeth thee to repentance?"

Ezekiel 33:11: "Say unto them, As I live, saith the Lord GOD, I have no pleasure in the death of the wicked; but that the wicked turn from his way and live: turn ye, turn ye from your evil ways; for why will ye die, O house of Israel?"

Ezekiel 18:23: "Have I any pleasure at all that the wicked should die? saith the Lord GOD: and not that he should return from his ways, and live?"

5. Which form of the common grace theory did the Christian Reformed Church adopt by this first declaration, the Kuyperian or the Arminian?

Virtually both; for, it is evident that, although they intended to adopt the Kuyperian theory only, they became confused when they attempted to support their view by the confession of the Reformed churches, and unwittingly they lapsed into the Arminian presentation of common grace.

6. *How could you prove this?*
This is evident, first of all, from the declaration itself. For, when it declares that "apart from the saving grace of God shown only to those that are elect unto eternal life, there is also a certain favor or grace of God which He shows to His creatures in general," it purposes to express the Kuyperian view that God is gracious to all men in common, elect and reprobate, godly and ungodly, when He bestows on them the things of this present life, such as rain and sunshine, life and health, wealth and possessions, gifts and talents. All the good things of this present time are, according to this view, a manifestation of God's gracious attitude to all men.

But the declaration lapses into the Arminian conception that the saving grace of God is intended for all men without exception, when it speaks of "the general offer of the gospel" as a manifestation of the grace of God to all the hearers without distinction. For it is evident that the gospel deals with saving grace.

The former theory we may designate by the term "common grace," for it speaks of a grace, not saving, that is *common* to the godly and the ungodly, the elect and the reprobate. The latter view is better expressed by the term "general grace," for it speaks of the grace of God, saving, that is intended for all men individually.

Both these views are clearly implied in the first point.

7. *From what else is it plain that the first point teaches both common and general grace?*
From the passages that are quoted from the confessions and from the Holy Scriptures in support of the first point. For, the first five texts quoted above are intended to prove the Kuyperian view of common grace. But the

last three texts, as well as the passages quoted from the confessions, do not deal with *common grace that is not saving,* but with *general grace that is saving as far as God's intention is concerned.*

8. Considering, then, first of all, the element of common grace as taught in the first point, is it not true that in this life the godly and the ungodly, the elect and reprobate have all things in common?

This is certainly true. There is manifestly in this world a general providence of God, by which the same things, both good and evil, rain and drought, abundance and scarcity, health and sickness, life and death, prosperity and adversity, peace and war, joy and sorrow, gifts, powers, talents, and genius or the want of these, occasions and seasons and times, are sent to men in common, regardless of the question whether they are godly or ungodly, just or unjust, elect or reprobate. We may even emphasize this by saying that both Scripture and experience teach that less good and more evils are sent to the godly than to the ungodly.

9. Is it, then, not also true that in the things of this present life both the godly and the ungodly receive tokens of God's favor toward them?

By no means; for, as it must be evident both from Scripture and experience that the evil things of this present life, such as sickness, pain, sorrow, adversity, poverty, yea, even death, are not sent to the godly in God's wrath and to curse them; so it must be evident that the good things of this present life are not sent to the wicked in God's favor and to bless them. We must not confuse *grace* and *things.*

10. In what light, then, must we consider the things which in this life the godly and the ungodly have in common, in

order correctly to evaluate them and understand their significance?

In the light of eternity. All the things of the present life are but means to an eternal end. As they are received by us and employed by us as rational-moral creatures they all bear fruit, either to eternal life and glory, or to eternal death and desolation. If they tend to life they are bestowed on us in the grace of God and are a blessing, no matter whether they are health or sickness, prosperity or adversity, life or death, for all things work together for good to them that love God; if they tend to death and damnation, they are bestowed on us in God's wrath and are a curse, even though our eyes stand out with fatness and we bathe in luxury.

11. Are, then, the things of this present life means in the hand of God or of men?

Both; as God employs them He carries out His eternal purpose concerning us, whether it be the purpose of salvation or of damnation; as we employ them as rational and moral beings, they become means of either righteousness or of unrighteousness. Thus God's counsel is realized concerning us and we remain moral and responsible agents.

12. But is it not possible to consider the temporal things apart from the eternal, and thus to maintain that in this life the ungodly enjoy many good things as tokens of God's grace toward them?

He that enjoys a nice sleigh-ride on a beautifully smooth and slippery road that ends in a deep precipice, or he that takes keen delight in a pleasant boat trip down the stream towards the Niagara Falls, would be considered a fool. So is he an abominable fool that considers the pleasures of this present time grace and a blessing though their end is inevitable destruction. You cannot separate the eternal from the temporal. All things are means to an end. It is, then, grace and a blessing to climb along a steep and rugged road to heaven; it is wrath and a curse to slide down a smooth road to hell.

13. But can we not truly say that God bestows the things of the present time upon the ungodly in His grace, though the wicked employ them unto their own destruction?

You would not ask this question from a Reformed viewpoint, nor if you are acquainted with the Word of God. For then you would know that God certainly and sovereignly predestinated both the elect and the reprobate unto their own end. He is God and not man. And as He predestinated their end, so He certainly predestinated the way and all the means to that end. Although, therefore, it is certainly true that the wicked, with all the means at their command, serve sin and work out their own destruction, yet it is equally true that they do so in full harmony with God's counsel and under His providence.

Besides, the viewpoint expressed in the question is contrary to the plain declarations of the Word of God, as we shall see later.

14. Do you, then, maintain that God is never gracious in time or eternity to the reprobate wicked?

I most emphatically maintain that this is true.

15. But is not this a terrible doctrine?

All true doctrine is terrible for the wicked and un-godly, for God is terrible to them. It is one of the earmarks of the falsity of the theory of common grace that it is pleasing to the ungodly. It is a great comfort to the godly, however, to know that all things work together for good to the righteous and for evil to the unrighteous. And it may rightly be characterized as an unethical, very cor-

rupt, and pernicious doctrine to teach that God favors the
workers of iniquity and smiles upon them in His grace!

16. Did not, then, synod of 1924 prove its contention on this point by the confessions?

Indeed not! They did not even make an attempt to
prove this part of the first point by statements from the
confessions of the Reformed churches. Evidently they
were quite aware that such an attempt would be utterly
futile. The statements from the confession which they do
quote are adduced to prove the Arminian element of the
first point. To this we must call attention later.

17. But do not the scriptural references quoted by synod corroborate the first point in its doctrine of common grace?

Superficially considered they would appear to do so.
However, a close examination of the passages will show
that the interpretation which synod would offer of them
is utterly false.

18. Does not Psalm 145:9 teach that God is gracious to the righteous and to the unrighteous reprobate?

Not at all. The word "all" in the sentence: "The Lord
is good to all," must be interpreted in the light of the
context. If we do so, it will at once be evident that it does
not mean "all men," godly and ungodly, but "all the
works of God," man and beast and the green tree and herb
of the field, the organic whole of creation, and that the
ungodly reprobate are exactly excluded from this "all."

19. How can you prove this?

First of all from the second part of the text: "and his
tender mercies are over all his works." According to the
well-known rule of Hebrew parallelism, of which we have
a plain illustration in this text, the second part here

explains the first. "All" in the first part is the same as "all his works" in the second part.

And, secondly, that this is indeed the correct interpretation of the text is corroborated by the last part of the psalm, where we read: "The LORD preserveth all them that love him, but all the wicked will he destroy" (v. 20).

20. But does not Matthew 5:44, 45 prove the point synod made in its first declaration?

If the synod's interpretation of this text were the correct one, it would prove far too much and, besides, it would lead to absurdity. It is deplorable that synod merely quoted, without even an attempt at explanation; otherwise synod would have soon realized how untenable is the position that in these verses we have a proof that God is gracious to all men. The interpretation which, evidently, synod would offer runs as follows:

a.   We must love our enemies.

b.   If we do, we will be children of God and reflect His love, for He loves all His enemies, as well as the good, in this present life.

c.   This love to all men is manifested in the rain and sunshine on all without distinction.

Of this interpretation we assert that, first, it proves too much and, secondly, it leads to absurdity and is untenable. It proves too much, for all the Scriptures witness that God does not love, but hates His enemies and purposes to destroy them, except those He chose in Christ Jesus and whom He loves, not as His enemies but as His redeemed people, justified and sanctified in Christ. God does, indeed, love His enemies, not as such, but as His children in Christ.

And it leads to absurdity, for if rain and sunshine are a manifestation of God's love to all men, the just and the unjust, what are floods and droughts, pestilences and earthquakes, and all destructive forces and evils sent to all through nature, but manifestations of His hatred for all, the just and the unjust? But it is absurd to say that God hates the just, for He loves them. It is also absurd to say that God changes, now loving the just and the unjust and manifesting this love in rain and sunshine, now hating them and revealing His hatred in upheavals and destruction. Hence, the interpretation that leads to this evident absurdity is itself absurd.

Besides, it must not be overlooked that the text does not at all state that God is gracious to the just and to the unjust, but that He rains and causes His sun to shine on all.

21. How, then, must the text be interpreted?

We must take our starting point from verse 44. The Lord admonishes His people that they shall love their enemies. Now, love is not a sentimental feeling or emotion or affection. It is, according to Scripture, the bond of perfectness (Col. 3:14). It is therefore the bond between two parties or persons who are ethically perfect, who seek each other and find delight in each other because of their ethical perfection, and who, in the sphere of ethical perfection, seek each other's good. It is in this true sense that God is love.

However, it stands to reason that, in the case of loving our enemies that despitefully use us, curse us, and persecute us, love must needs be one-sided. There cannot be a bond of fellowship between the wicked and the perfect in Christ. To love our enemy, therefore, is not to flatter him, to have fellowship with him, to play games with him, and to speak sweetly to him; but rather to rebuke him, to demand that he leave his wicked way, and thus to bless him and to pray for him. It is to bestow good things upon him with the demand of true love that he leave his wicked way, walk in the light, and thus have fellowship with us.

If he heed our love, which will be the case if he be of God's elect and receive grace, he will turn from darkness into light, and our love will assume the nature of a bond of perfectness. If he despise our love, our very act of love will be to his greater damnation. But the cursing and persecution of the wicked may never tempt the child of God to live and act from the principle of hatred, to reward evil for evil, an eye for an eye and a tooth for a tooth.

As a single illustration from actual life and experience, the Lord points to the fact that so God rains and causes His sun to shine upon the just and the unjust, thus bestowing good things upon them all, demanding that they shall employ them as means to walk in righteousness and light. For with God love is delight in perfection in the highest sense of the word. If now the wicked receive grace with rain and sunshine, they will walk in the light and have fellowship with God. If they do not receive grace, they will employ the rain and the sunshine in the service of sin and receive the greater damnation.

But rain and sunshine are never grace and Matthew 5:44, 45 does not prove the contention of the first point.

22. But does not Luke 6:35, 36 plainly speak of God being kind to the unthankful and evil?

This text is far more simple than that of Matthew 5, because it merely speaks of the unthankful and evil. No one denies that God is kind to the unthankful and evil. Only, He is not kind to the reprobate unthankful and evil. The entire context of Luke 6:35, 36 shows clearly that the Lord purposes to teach:

    a. That His own people tasted the goodness and the kindness of God toward them while they were and often still are unthankful and evil.

    b. That, having tasted the love of God as a love that reveals itself as grace and kindness toward the

unthankful and evil, they must reveal that same kindness toward their enemies, lending and giving without ever hoping to receive again.

That God loves and is gracious to the ungodly in
Christ does not at all prove that He loves and is gracious
to all the ungodly, even those that are outside of Christ.

**23. Does not the text from Acts 14:16, 17 teach that God
is gracious to the reprobate ungodly?**
Evidently not; for:
a.   It merely teaches that God did not leave Himself
without a witness to the heathen world even in the old
dispensation.   He revealed Himself as the One who
must be thanked and served, for He did good from
heaven, giving rain and fruitful seasons, filling them
with food and gladness.   And, naturally, by means of
these testimonies the heathen knew that God was to
be thanked and served.

b.   However, the text states plainly that God let them
walk in their own sinful ways, the ways of iniquity
and destruction.   Though they knew God and received His witness, they received no grace; and with
their rain, fruitful seasons, and food and gladness
they served sin and were objects of His wrath and
damnation. Fruitful seasons, food and gladness, with
material things are not grace, neither are they a manifestation of grace.

24. And how must I Timothy 4:10 be explained?
Either:
a.   Savior in the text means Preserver, as the synod of
1924 evidently understood the word and the Dutch
translation renders it.   In that case the text does not
speak of grace at all, but merely of God's providential
preservation of all men, the wicked as well as the

righteous, the reprobate as well as the elect. The text then means: God is a Preserver of all men, for He gives to all men their existence and life and all things necessary for the sustenance of their being; but especially of believers, for them and them only He preserves in His grace, leading them to eternal life.

Or:

b.   Savior has the usual meaning of Deliverer from sin and death. In that case the text means: God is a Savior of all men — more specifically speaking, of believers from among all men.

But whichever interpretation is preferred, the text does not support the theory of a common grace of God toward and upon the godly and the ungodly, the elect and the reprobate.

The General Grace Theory of the First Point

1. Will you mention again the distinction you made between common and general grace?

By common grace is meant the grace of God, not saving, *common* both to the elect and the reprobate, the godly and the ungodly, alleged to be manifest in the things of this present time as they are common to all men. By general grace the theory is denoted that holds that the saving grace of God is *general,* i.e., intended for all men without exception. The latter theory is a denial of sovereign election and reprobation and of particular atonement and teaches that Christ died for all, but that the application of His atoning death depends upon the choice of the will of the sinner.

2. In what part of the first point do you find the element of general grace?

In the last part. There it teaches that it is evident from the general offer of the gospel that there is a certain favor or grace of God over His creatures in general. This is also the intention of the implied exegesis of such texts as Romans 2:4; Ezekiel 33:11; 18:23, quoted by synod to prove their contention.

3. How would you briefly and concisely formulate this part of the first point?

Thus: In the preaching of the gospel God is graciously

inclined and bestows grace upon all the hearers. Or, still more briefly: The preaching of the gospel is grace to all.

4. And what is the true Reformed and scriptural view?
That the preaching of the gospel is, both in God's intention and in actual application, grace to the elect only, while it is a savor of death unto death for the reprobate.

5. Can you briefly outline the true Reformed and biblical truth of particular grace?
Yes; it contains the following elements:

a. From all eternity God sovereignly loved and chose a people in Christ, ordaining them unto eternal glory through the deep way of sin and grace.

b. In their stead and in their behalf Christ, whom God sent in the likeness of sinful flesh, suffered and died, arose from the dead, and was glorified at the right hand of God, thus meriting for the elect, given Him by the Father, and for them only, all the blessings of salvation.

c. By the Spirit of grace the elect, and they only, are regenerated, called into the fellowship of Jesus Christ efficaciously and irresistibly; upon them is bestowed the saving grace whereby they believe in Christ as He is proclaimed unto them in the gospel, whereby they are justified and sanctified and glorified.

d. By the same efficacious grace they are preserved unto final salvation, and they can never fall away from grace but will surely persevere even unto the end, when God will glorify them and make them heirs of all things with Jesus Christ their Lord.

e. Hence, the preaching of the gospel is, neither in God's intention nor in actual fact, grace to all the hearers, but only to the elect for whom Christ died and rose again, and whom God through that preaching effectually calls unto eternal life and glory.

6. Is the above outline actually the teaching of the Reformed confessions?

It certainly is; and it is taught throughout all the standards of the Reformed churches.

7. Will you quote some passages from the confessions in proof of this last statement?

Yes:

Canons of Dordrecht, I, A, 6: "That some receive the gift of faith from God, and others do not receive it proceeds from God's eternal decree, 'For known unto God are all his works from the beginning of the world,' (Acts 15:18). 'Who worketh all things after the counsel of his will' (Eph. 1:11). According to which decree he graciously softens the hearts of the elect, however obstinate, and inclines them to believe, while he leaves the non-elect in his just judgment to their own wickedness and obduracy. And herein is especially displayed the profound, the merciful, and at the same time the righteous discrimination between men, equally involved in ruin; or that decree of election and reprobation, revealed in the Word of God which though men of perverse, impure and unstable minds wrest to their own destruction, yet to holy and pious souls affords unspeakable consolation."

Canons of Dordrecht, II, A, 8: "For this was the sovereign counsel, and most gracious will and purpose of God the Father, that the quickening and saving efficacy of the most precious death of his Son should extend to all the elect, for bestowing upon them alone the gift of justifying faith, thereby to bring them infallibly to salvation: that is, it was the will of God, that Christ, by the blood of the cross, whereby he confirmed the new covenant, should effectually redeem out of every people, tribe, nation, and language, all those, and those only, who were from eternity chosen to salvation, and given to him by the Father; that he should confer upon them faith, which together with all the other saving gifts of the Holy Spirit, he purchased for them by his death; should purge them from all sin, both original and actual, whether committed before or after believing; and having faithfully preserved them even to the end, should at last bring them free from every spot and blemish to the enjoyment of glory in his own presence forever."

Canons of Dordrecht, III/IV, A, 10: "But that others who are called by the gospel, obey the call, and are converted, is not to be ascribed to the proper exercise of free will, whereby one distinguishes himself above others, equally furnished with grace sufficient for faith and conversions, as the proud heresy of Pelagius maintains; but it must be wholly ascribed to God, who as he has chosen his own from eternity in Christ, so he confers upon them faith and repentance, rescues them from the power of darkness, and translates them into the kingdom of his own Son, that they may show forth the praises of him, who hath called them out of darkness into his marvelous light; and may glory not in themselves, but in the Lord according to the testimony of the apostles in various places."

Canons of Dordrecht, V, A, 8: "Thus, it is not in consequence of their own merits, or strength, but of God's free mercy, that they do not totally fall from faith and grace, nor continue and perish finally in their backslidings; which, with respect to themselves, is not only possible, but would undoubtedly happen; but with respect to God, it is utterly impossible, since his counsel cannot be changed, nor his promise fail, neither can the call according to his purpose be revoked, nor the merit, intercession and preservation of Christ be rendered ineffectual, nor the sealing of the Holy Spirit be frustrated or obliterated."

8. *Is the above-mentioned doctrine sustained by Scripture?*

Yes; abundantly so and in many passages.

9. *Will you mention some passages?*
Yes:

Romans 8:29, 30: "For whom he did foreknow, he also did predestinate to be conformed to the image of his Son, that he might be the firstborn among many brethren. Moreover whom he did predestinate, them he also called: and whom he called, them he also justified: and whom he justified, them he also glorified."

Romans 9:13: "As it is written, Jacob have I loved, but Esau have I hated."

Romans 9:18: "Therefore hath he mercy on whom he will have mercy, and whom he will he hardeneth."

Romans 9:16: "So then it is not of him that willeth, nor of him that runneth, but of God that sheweth mercy."

Ephesians 1:3, 4: "Blessed be the God and Father of our Lord Jesus Christ, who hath blessed us with all spiritual blessings in heavenly places in Christ: according as he hath chosen us in him before the foundation of the world, that we should be holy and without blame before him in love."

John 6:37: "All that the Father giveth me shall come to me; and him that cometh to me I will in no wise cast out."

John 6:65: "And he said, Therefore said I unto you, that no man can come unto me, except it were given unto him of my Father."

John 10:26-30: "But ye believe not, because ye are not of my sheep, as I said unto you. My sheep hear my voice, and I know them, and they follow me: and I give unto them eternal life; and they shall never perish, neither shall any man pluck them out of my hand. My Father, which gave them me, is greater than all; and no man is able to pluck them out of my Father's hand. I and my Father are one."

I Peter 1:4, 5: "To an inheritance incorruptible, and undefiled, and that fadeth not away, reserved in heaven for you, who are kept by the power of God through faith unto salvation ready to be revealed in the last time."

10. But, granting the truth of all this, is it not a fact that the gospel is preached to many that are not elect and are not saved?

Most certainly. It would be quite impossible to preach the gospel to the elect only; neither is this the will of God, for the Scriptures declare that many are called but few are chosen.

11. And, if this be conceded, is it not also true that this preaching of the gospel must be regarded as a token and offer of God's grace to all that hear the gospel?

By no means. On the contrary, the Scriptures teach plainly that the preaching of the gospel is a savor of death unto death to the reprobate, according to the righteous judgment of God.

12. Where does the Bible teach this?

In many places.

13. Will you quote a few passages?

Certainly.

II Corinthians 2:15, 16: "For we are unto God a sweet savour of Christ, in them that are saved, and in them that perish: to the one we are the savour of death unto death; and to the other the savour of life unto life. And who is sufficient for these things?"

Mark 4:11, 12: "And he said unto them, Unto you it is given to know the mystery of the kingdom of God: but unto them that are without, all these things are done in parables: that seeing they may see, and not perceive; and hearing they may hear, and not understand; lest at any time they should be converted, and their sins should be forgiven them."

Matthew 11:25, 26: "At that time Jesus answered and said, I thank thee, O Father, Lord of heaven and earth, because thou hast hid these things from the wise and prudent, and hast revealed them unto babes. Even so, Father: for so it seemed good in thy sight." Remember that Jesus spoke these words with reference to those among whom He had preached the gospel and performed His wonderful works.

John 12:39, 40: "Therefore they could not believe, because that Esaias said again, he hath blinded their eyes, and hardened their heart; that they should not see with their eyes, nor understand with their heart, and be converted, and I should heal them."

I Peter 2:7, 8: "Unto you therefore which believe he is precious: but unto them which be disobedient, the stone which the builders disallowed, the same is made the head of the corner, and a stone of stumbling, and a rock of offence, even to them which stumble at the word, being disobedient: whereunto also they were appointed."

14. Do the confessions also have something to say on this point?

Yes; for, in Canons II, B, 6 they reject the errors of those "who use the difference between meriting and appropriating, to the end that they may instill into the minds of the imprudent and inexperienced this teaching that God, as far as he is concerned, has been minded of applying to all equally the benefits gained by the death of Christ; but that, while some obtain the pardon of sin and eternal life, and others do not, this difference depends on their own free will, which joins itself to the grace that is offered

without exception, and that it is not dependent on the
special gift of mercy, which powerfully works in them,
that they rather than others should appropriate unto
themselves this grace. For these, while they feign that
they present this distinction, in a sound sense, seek to
instill into the people the destructive poison of the Pelagian
errors."

**15. But did you not say that also the synod of 1924
quoted from the same confessions in support of their
contention that the preaching of the gospel is grace to all
that hear?**
    Yes, I did; synod quoted from Canons of Dordrecht,
II, 5 and III/IV, 8 and 9. In the preceding chapter we
quoted them in full.

16. What do the confessions teach in Canons II, 5?
    It teaches especially three things:
    a.   That the promise of the gospel must be preached
promiscuously to all nations and men without distinction.

    b.   That it is, however, the good pleasure of God that
determines even where that gospel shall be preached.

    c.   That, as to its contents, this promise of the gospel
is that whosoever believeth in Christ crucified shall
not perish, but have everlasting life.
    Surely, this presents the promise of the gospel as
strictly particular, for it is to them that believe in Christ,
that is, the elect. The gospel is not presented here as a
general offer. Still less does this part of our confession
teach that the preaching of the gospel is grace of God to all
that hear it. Synod was utterly mistaken.

**17. And what do the confessions teach in Canons III/IV,
8?**

Again, especially three things:

a.   That the calling by the gospel is unfeigned. This calling of the gospel is to repent and believe. God is serious, of course, when through the gospel He sends this calling to any man. For no man has the right before God to remain in his sin and live in unbelief.

b.   That God reveals, therefore, in the gospel, that it is pleasing to Him that they that are called should come unto Him.

c.   That He seriously promises eternal life and rest to as many as believe and come unto Him.

Again, this promise is strictly particular, for it is to them that believe and come to God in Christ, that is, the elect. There is not a trace in the article of the doctrine that the preaching of the gospel is grace to all the hearers.

18. And what is the teaching of Canons III/IV, 9?

That the fault and guilt of the rejection of the gospel by the reprobate is not God's, nor Christ's, nor the gospel's, but wholly the sinner's.

19. But does not this article teach that Christ is offered in the gospel?

It does; but it must be remembered that "offer" has here the meaning of "present." Christ is indeed, in the preaching of the gospel, presented to all who hear. But this presentation or offering of Christ is not grace to all who hear. This article does not even suggest such a thing.

20. But did not the synod also quote from the Scriptures in support of their declaration?

Yes, they did. They quoted Romans 2:4; Ezekiel 18:23; 33:11. For the full quotation of these texts we refer you to the previous chapter.

21. What interpretation of Romans 2:4 did synod evidently favor?

The thoroughly Arminian interpretation that God intended to lead man to repentance by the manifestation of His goodness and forbearance and longsuffering, but that man refused and, despising these riches of the goodness of God, perished. This is also the interpretation of Professor L. Berkhof in his booklet on the Three Points.

22. What would you say of this interpretation from an exegetical viewpoint?

That it is quite impossible and wholly contrary to the plain words of the text. The text does not say that it is the *intention* of God in the manifestation of the divine virtues enumerated to lead to repentance, but that it actually *leads* to repentance. The apostle plainly writes: "not knowing that the goodness of God *leadeth thee to repentance.*" This is not to be changed into: intendeth to lead thee to repentance.

23. But how, then, would you interpret the text?

Paul is addressing man. (See vv. 1 and 3.) Now, the evident question is, how Paul could write of the same man, that God's goodness *leads* him to repentance, while on the other hand, he does not know this, despises this goodness, and gathers unto himself treasures of wrath. It is very clear that this could not possibly be asserted of the same individual. For, if the goodness of God leadeth a man to repentance, he does not despise that goodness, and if he despises the goodness of God, that goodness does not lead him to repentance. The two are mutually exclusive. Hence, the solution of this question must be sought in the fact that the apostle is not addressing an individual, but a class. Man must be understood collectively. It is true, that the goodness of God leadeth man to repentance, that is, the elect man. It is also true, that man despiseth this goodness of God, and that he gathers for himself treasures of wrath, not knowing that the goodness of God leadeth man to repentance. This last predicate is true of the ungodly reprobate.

24. But do not Ezekiel 18:23 and 33:11 teach that God is gracious in the preaching of the gospel to the reprobate wicked?

This is surely the interpretation of the synod of 1924, as well as of Professor L. Berkhof in his booklet written in defense of the Three Points. But notice, with regard to these two texts, which are essentially the same in meaning:

a.   That in neither of these passages is there any offer of grace or salvation at all, as far as the form of the texts is concerned. In both passages we have a direct statement by the Lord, the God of Israel, that He hath no pleasure in the death of the wicked, but therein that he turn and live. In the text from chapter 33 this statement stands in the form of an oath. It is, therefore, no offer, but a most emphatic divine assertion.

b.   That in both the texts it is the house of Israel that is addressed. The Lord, therefore, through His prophet does not address the wicked in general, but the church, those who are called His people, those whom He chooses, but who have departed from the way of the covenant of the Lord. This certainly does not plead in favor of the interpretation that would apply this text to the reprobate wicked, or to elect and reprobate alike. It is His people whom the Lord assures of His forgiving mercy.

c.   This is corroborated by the context, especially of the text in chapter 33:11. There the assertion of forgiving grace by the Lord is an answer to the complaint of the people of God: "If our transgressions and our sins be upon us, and we pine away in them, how should we then live?" They were conscious of their sin. They felt that they were worthy of condemnation and death because of their transgressions. And they did not see a way out. They did not understand that the Lord is abundant in tender mercy and forgiving grace. They pined away in their sin, and they must surely die. To these people the Lord answers that there is abundant hope. For He hath no pleasure in the death of His people, even when they have departed from His ways. He will have mercy on them and forgive. Therefore, let them turn, and He will pardon, and they shall live.

d.   Finally, notice that the Lord has no pleasure in the death of the wicked that turns and lives. Scripture elsewhere frequently testifies that the Lord does have a holy pleasure in the destruction of the wicked. For He hates all the workers of iniquity, and He shall laugh in their destruction and hold them in derision. But the Lord does have pleasure that the wicked turn from their evil way. And when they turn from their wicked way and are wicked no more, He delights in their life, and gives it unto them abundantly by His grace.

From all these elements it ought to be very evident that the texts cannot be applied to the reprobate wicked; and, surely, that there is no general offer of grace in these passages from Ezekiel.

Sundry Arguments Refuted

1. But are there not, besides the references made by synod, many passages in Scripture that plainly teach a general offer of salvation which is grace to all the hearers?

I do not know of any. However, those that teach such a general offer erroneously appeal to many texts. These passages usually contain either a *calling,* with a promise to them that hear and heed it; or some general word such as "all" or "world," the real meaning of which must be determined by the context.

2. Does not Scripture teach in John 3:16: "For God so loved the world, that he gave his only begotten Son, that whosoever believeth in him should not perish, but have everlasting life"?

Certainly; but notice:

a.   That in this text there is not only no general offer of grace and salvation, but there is no offer at all. The passage contains a statement concerning God. As the introductory word "for" indicates plainly, it adduces a reason for the immediately preceding verse, which emphasizes the *necessity* of the lifting up of the Son of man. Christ *must* be lifted up on the cross and into glory. Why? Because God so loved the world that He gave His only begotten Son. Surely it must be admitted that the love of God is sovereign and unchangeable. If He loves someone with the love by which He gave His only begotten Son, that one will surely be saved.

b. That the object of this love of God is "the world." But "world" occurs with different connotations in Scripture. The meaning must be determined from the text or from its context. Fact is, however, that it never means "all men without exception." This is neither the meaning of the word itself nor does the word ever have this meaning in the context in which it occurs. Let us consider some of these meanings:

1) The most natural meaning of "world" or *kosmos* is creation in its organic sense, either as it actually exists, or as God conceived of the whole of His works in their final perfection in His counsel before the foundation of the world. It refers to the works of God as one whole, harmoniously related, without having respect to individual creatures. Creation, as it consummates in man, stands and falls with man and will be redeemed and glorified with man in the believers or the elect. This is the meaning of the word in John 3:16. That world, the whole of God's works, as it will be glorified and redeemed in and with the elect believers, is the object of that love of God by which He gave His only begotten Son. Hence, not all men in the world, but "whosoever believeth on Him" shall be saved and have eternal life.

2) The word "world" may also mean this present world as it is in sin and corruption. Even then the original sense of "creation," or the whole of the works of God, is not entirely absent from it, but it looks at these works of God from the viewpoint of their being dominated by the wicked, so that all things are pressed into the service of sin. Also, the wicked commit their iniquity and develop in sin in

connection with and by means of God's creation. Hence, they are "the world," and the forms of life they create in their sin are also "the world." In this sense we must understand the word in John 17:9, where the Lord says: "I pray for them: I pray not for the world, but for them which thou hast given me; for they are thine." Thus also in John 17:16: "They are not of the world, even as I am not of the world." And again in I John 2:15-17: "Love not the world, neither the things that are in the world. If any man love the world, the love of the Father is not in him. For all that is in the world, the lust of the flesh, and the lust of the eyes, and the pride of life, is not of the Father, but is of the world. And the world passeth away, and the lust thereof: but he that doeth the will of God abideth forever." It is also in this sense that the word is used when Scripture calls the devil "the prince of this world" (John 14:30; 16:11).

3) The world may also mean the totality of the saved out of the world, because the saved are gathered from every nation and tongue and tribe and not merely from a single nation or group. A plain illustration of this connotation you will find in II Corinthians 5:19: "To wit, that God was in Christ, reconciling the world unto himself, not imputing their trespasses unto them; and hath committed unto us the word of reconciliation." They that would interpret the word "world" in this text as meaning *all men* must needs distort and deny the true meaning of the word "reconciliation." To reconcile always implies the blotting out of sin. That this is also implied in the text is evident from the words "not imputing their trespasses unto them." It is clear, then, that this "world" is

actually saved in the blood of Christ. It *is* recon-
ciled. But, then, either of these is true: "world"
does not mean "all men," or "all men" are saved.
The latter is not true; hence, "world" does not
signify *all men,* but the totality of the saved out of
every nation. Another illustration of this meaning
of the word "world" you may find in I John 2:2:
"And he is the propitiation for our sins: and not for
ours only (that is, for us, as we have already been
called as a church), but also for the sins of the
whole world (all the saved as they shall be called
out of every nation)."

**3. But does not the Bible teach in II Peter 3:9 that God
will not that any should perish, but that all should come
to repentance?**

It does; but whenever you read this word "all" in
Scripture you must carefully study the text to determine
the contents of this term. Unless the text or the context
plainly indicates the contrary, the word "all" does not
mean "all men" or the whole of the number of men that
ever lived or live and shall live on earth.

a. It may mean: "all of us," i.e., of the church. This
is plainly the meaning in the text from II Peter 3:9. For
the entire text reads: "The Lord is not slack concerning his promise, as some men count slackness; but is
longsuffering to *usward,* not willing that any should
perish, but that all should come to repentance." That
"all" here means "all of us," or the church, is evident
from:

1) the text itself; God is longsuffering to *usward,*
not willing that any *of us* should perish;

2) the fact that the promise would never be fulfilled and Christ would never come again, if the

text would mean "all men must first come to repentance," for they never will;

3) the fact that God's will is certainly realized; if He does not will that we should perish, we surely shall be saved.

b. It may also mean: "all kinds of men." This is plainly the meaning in Titus 2:11: "For the grace of God that bringeth salvation hath appeared to all men." That "all men" cannot mean every individual of the human race, nor every man then living, ought to be evident from the meaning of the text. The apostle writes that the grace of God that bringeth salvation had, in his day, already appeared to all men. It is a fact, however, that comparatively few had as yet heard the gospel, so that "all men" cannot possibly signify every living man in the world of that time. And that it does mean "all kinds of men" is evident from the fact that the text states a reason for sundry exhortations that occur in the context. In that context the apostle mentions aged men and aged women, young men and young women, servants and masters, i.e., different classes of people; *for*, he continues, the grace of God that bringeth salvation hath appeared to all men, that is, to men of every station in life. This is also the meaning of "all men" in I Timothy 2:4, as the context plainly shows.

c. "All" may also simply mean "all believers" or "all the elect." This is plainly the case in I Corinthians 15:22: "For as in Adam all die, even so in Christ shall all be made alive." It is indisputable that the second "all" cannot mean "all men"; for these "all" shall be made alive in the glorious resurrection of Christ, which is not true of all men, but only of all believers or of the elect. Of these the apostle is speaking. This is also true of the word "all" in John 12:32: "And I, if I be

lifted up from the earth, will draw all men unto me."
The word *men* does not occur in the original of this
verse. It is plain that whom Christ *draws* unto Him are
surely saved. Hence, the simple meaning is: I will
draw all My own, all the elect, unto Me.

d. Sometimes "all men" must be interpreted as meaning "all of one group" in distinction from "all of
another group." This is the case in Romans 5:18:
"Therefore, as by the offence of one judgment came
upon all men to condemnation; even so by the righteousness of one the free gift came upon all men unto
justification of life." You must note that in the latter
part of this text it does not say that the free gift is
offered to all men, but that it *came* upon all men unto
justification of life. Now, they who actually receive
this free gift are surely saved. Hence, they cannot be
all men without exception. But they do include "all
that belong to the group of which Christ is the Head"
in distinction from "the group of which Adam is the
head."

Thus, you must remember that the word "all" has
sundry meanings, and that its specific meaning in any
one text must be determined from the text itself and from
its context. Then you will not easily be led astray from the
truth by those who quote such texts at random.

**4. But is there no general offer of grace in the words of
Christ: "Come unto me, all ye that labor and are heavy
laden, and I will give you rest"?**

By no means; for:

a. It must not be overlooked that Christ here calls
those that labor and are heavy laden. They are such in
the same sense as that in which He promised them
rest, i.e., in the spiritual sense. Although, therefore,
the preaching of this calling is general, its content is,
evidently, particular.

b. The Lord does not preach a general offer in these words, but a very specific and particular promise. He promises rest to them that come unto Him. And these are the elect, for no man can come to Him except the Father draw him.

5. Why, then, does the Bible say that Christ stands at the door of a man's heart and knocks? Surely this presupposes that He is willing to come in if man but opens the door of his heart.

I confess that I do not know of any text that speaks of Christ's knocking at the door of man's heart.

6. But does not Scripture teach this in Revelation 3:20: "Behold, I stand at the door, and knock"?

Let me call your attention to the fact that the text does not speak of the door of man's heart, as if the door were locked from the inside and must be opened by man if Christ is to come in. It must be admitted that the text does not define what door is meant. This, then, must be determined from the context if possible. Nor is this difficult, for according to the context Christ is addressing, not any individual, but the church of Laodicea. It stands to reason, therefore, that the door of this church is meant in verse 20. Christ represents Himself as standing *outside* of that church, for it is a thoroughly apostate church. Christ is about to spew her out of His mouth. Yet even in that church of Laodicea there is a remnant according to the election, be it ever so small. They must come out, and Christ will recognize them as the church, for He promises that He will sup with them. And thus the text must be read: Behold, I stand at the door of the church and knock!

7. Does not the Bible teach a general offer of salvation, when it says: "whosoever will may come"?

I am afraid that you quote this from a hymn rather than from the Word of God.

8. But are not these words found in Revelation 22:17?
No; there you read the following words: "And the Spirit and the bride say, Come. And let him that heareth say, Come. And let him that is athirst come. And whosoever will, let him take the water of life freely."
Now, notice:
a.   That the text first of all speaks of him that is athirst. Athirst after what? After the water of life, of course. It speaks, therefore, to them that are truly, spiritually athirst. And this is not true of all men, though they may thirst after many things. They surely do not thirst after the living God.

b.   That it is only he that is athirst that *will* take of the water of life. He that is not athirst will not take that water, but he despises it. The will to take of the water of life is motivated by the thirst. Hence, "whosoever will" and "he that is athirst" are identical. Christ, therefore, calls whosoever is athirst.

c.   But this being athirst, and therefore also this will to take of the water of life freely, is not of nature, but of the grace of God. God is always first, not man. From which it follows that also in Revelation 22:17 the Lord is calling the elect by their spiritual name.

9. Does the Bible also directly deny that the preaching of the gospel is grace to all that hear?
It most emphatically does in many places. And not only this, but it teaches positively that the preaching of the Word is a savor of life unto life and a savor of death unto death according to the will and purpose of God.

10. *Where does the Bible teach this?*

In Isaiah 6:9, 10: "And he said, Go, and tell this people, Hear ye indeed, but understand not; and see ye indeed, but perceive not. Make the heart of this people fat, and make their ears heavy, and shut their eyes; lest they see with their eyes, and hear with their ears, and understand with their heart, and convert, and be healed."

11. *In what other passage does Scripture teach the same truth?*

In Mark 4:11, 12: "And he said unto them, Unto you it is given to know the mystery of the kingdom of God: but unto them that are without, all these things are done in parables: that seeing they may see, and not perceive; and hearing they may hear, and not understand; lest at any time they should be converted, and their sins should be forgiven them."

12. *Does Scripture attribute this twofold effect of the preaching of the gospel to God's will and purpose?*

It does in Matthew 11:25-27: "At that time Jesus answered and said, I thank thee, O Father, Lord of heaven and earth, because thou hast hid these things from the wise and prudent, and hast revealed them unto babes. Even so, Father: for so it seemed good in thy sight. All things are delivered unto me of my Father; and no man knoweth the Son, but the Father; neither knoweth any man the Father, save the Son, and he to whomsoever the Son will reveal him."

13. *What other passage teaches this same truth?*

John 12:39, 40: "Therefore they could not believe, because that Esaias said again, he hath blinded their eyes, and hardened their heart; that they should not see with their eyes, nor understand with their heart, and be converted, and I should heal them."

14. Can you mention still another text?

Yes, II Corinthians 2:14-16: "Now thanks be unto God, which always causeth us to triumph in Christ, and maketh manifest the savour of his knowledge by us in every place. For we are unto God a sweet savour of Christ, in them that are saved, and in them that perish: to the one we are the savour of death unto death; and to the other the savour of life unto life. And who is sufficient for these things?"

15. But does not this doctrine make God the author of sin?

This is often alleged by those who are enemies of the truth of God's absolutely sovereign grace. For awhile they will reason with you from and on the basis of the Word of God. When, however, they must admit that Scripture is all against them and throughout teaches the sovereignty of the Most High, they abandon this only safe method of argumentation in order to shoot their own poisoned arrows at what is admittedly scriptural truth. Scripture answers all such objections by putting man where he belongs, that is, prostrate in the dust, when it says: "Nay but, O man, who art thou that repliest against God?" (Rom. 9:20).

And to them that sincerely seek the truth in this matter, the following may be said in answer to their question. God is not the author of sin, and far be it from us even to imagine such wickedness. For He is holy and pure, a light and there is no darkness in Him. But although He is not the *author* of sin, which would imply that He finds pleasure in it and commits sin, He is the ultimate Cause of all things and, therefore, also of the *fact* of sin. This distinction, then, must be made, that not God but man is the *author* of the *deed* of sin, while God is the ultimate *Cause* of the *fact* of sin. In His counsel God wills the fact of sin, in order that it might become manifest that

He hates sin and might reveal His righteousness. Besides, it must not be forgotten that God makes sin and the wicked subservient to the purpose of leading His elect to the highest glory of the heavenly kingdom.

16. Do you, however, by so strictly maintaining the sovereignty of God over all things, not deny the responsibility of man?

That we do is only another accusation made against us by those who oppose the truth of sovereign grace. All these objections are not of a recent date but are as old as the truth itself. They are only raised with a new emphasis when the doctrine of God's absolute sovereignty is given its proper place. And also with regard to this objection we must remember that it contains no argument from Scripture. The Word of God plainly teaches God's sovereignty over all things, and "who art thou, O man, that repliest against God?"

As to the question itself, we must understand, first of all, that responsibility does not and cannot presuppose sovereign freedom. There is only one who is sovereignly free, namely God. The creature is dependent even in his moral life. In the second place, we must see that a creature is responsible when he acts as a moral agent, that is, when he consciously and willingly performs that which he does. He always says "Yes" and "No" with respect to God and sin, according to the inner choice of his heart. He remains, therefore, the author of his works. He is always a moral agent. And, finally, we must remember that God's providential rule even over the heart of man is never of such a nature that it violates this moral character of man. While God, therefore, alone is sovereign and reigns even over all the deeds and purposes of man, so that His counsel is executed, He deals with man according to his nature, that is, as a moral agent. The *manner* of this operation of God may be too deep for us to search out and comprehend; the *fact* itself is plainly revealed in the Word of God.

17. But is not the preaching of this doctrine dangerous, seeing that it tends to make men careless and profane?

If we should answer this question affirmatively, we would thereby criticize the Word of God itself, for it declares this doctrine openly in the most emphatic terms.

Nor is this true. For, while by nature we are all careless and profane, in the sense that we are enemies of God; and while the reprobate wicked remain such to their own condemnation; it is impossible that a heart that is touched by the grace of God and brought into a saving contact with the Lord Jesus Christ should assume an attitude of indifference over against God and His covenant. For this grace of God makes men desirous to walk in all good works to the glory of Him who called them out of darkness into His marvelous light.

18. But does not this doctrine kill every incentive to mission work?

They who raise this supercilious objection do so only because they are still entangled in a network of Arminian errors and also have an Arminian conception of the real nature of mission work. And it may readily be admitted that the truth of God's sovereign grace is opposed to all such mission work as proceeds from the notion that it purposes to save men by man's effort.

However, if you understand that the positive purpose of mission work cannot be anything else than to gather the church, chosen unto eternal life from among all nations and tongues and tribes, the doctrine of God's sovereign grace is not only no objection to, but is the only possible and sound basis from which one can proceed to do mission work. For now we have His own promise, that "all that the Father giveth me shall come to me; and him that cometh to me I will in no wise cast out" (Jn. 6:37).

The Second Point
and Its Implications

1. What do you mean by the "second point"?

The second of the three doctrinal declarations adopted and added to the confessions of the Christian Reformed Church by their synod of 1924.

2. Can you quote it?

Certainly; it is as follows: "Relative to the second point, which is concerned with the restraint of sin in the life of the individual man and in the community, the synod declares that there is such a restraint of sin according to Scripture and the Confession. This is evident from the citations from Scripture and from the Netherlands Confession, Articles 13 and 36, which teach that God by the general operations of His Spirit, without renewing the heart of man, restrains the unimpeded breaking out of sin, by which human life in society remains possible; while it is also evident from the quotations from Reformed writers of the most flourishing period of Reformed theology, that from ancient times our Reformed fathers were of the same opinion."

3. To which passages from the confession does synod refer in support of this declaration?

To Article 13 of the Belgic Confession, particularly to the following sentence: "in whom we do entirely trust;

101

being persuaded, that he so restrains the devil and all our enemies, that without his will and permission, they cannot hurt us."

And to the following quotation from Article 36: "willing that the world should be governed by certain laws and policies; to the end that the dissoluteness of men might be restrained."

4. What proof from Scripture does synod adduce in support of the second point?

The following:

Genesis 6:3: "And the LORD said, My Spirit shall not always strive with man."

Psalm 81:11, 12: "But my people would not hearken to my voice; and Israel would none of me. So I gave them up unto their own hearts' lust: and they walked in their own counsels."

Acts 7:42: "Then God turned, and gave them up to worship the host of heaven; as it is written in the book of the prophets, O ye house of Israel, have ye offered to me slain beasts and sacrifices by the space of forty years in the wilderness?"

Romans 1:24: "Wherefore God also gave them up to uncleanness through the lusts of their own hearts, to dishonour their own bodies between themselves."

Romans 1:26: "For this cause God gave them up unto vile affections: for even their women did change the natural use into that which is against nature."

Romans 1:28: "And even as they did not like to retain God in their knowledge, God gave them over to a reprobate mind, to do those things which are not convenient."

II Thessalonians 2:6, 7: "And now ye know what withholdeth that he might be revealed in his time. For the mystery of iniquity doth already work: only he who now letteth will let, until he be taken out of the way."

5. *Does the second point merely teach that the sinner is restrained, limited, and controlled in his outward actions, so that he cannot fully execute and always carry out his evil intentions?*

By no means. For this is a thoroughly Reformed doctrine. We all understand and heartily confess that God holds in His power and perfectly controls by His providence all the deeds of the wicked, both devils and men, so that they cannot accomplish anything against His will. He does this directly by His power, frequently frustrating the counsels of the ungodly in a way which is even beyond our comprehension, for their very thoughts and desires are in His hand and under His control. But He also controls and restrains the wicked indirectly and mediately. The ungodly are dependent on and limited by time and occasion and circumstances; by their place and position in life; by their talents and power and means; by their own ambitions and fears and by the powers that be; yea, they are limited by their own character and disposition. This outward restraint of the sinner no one denies. But it is not this external restraint of the sinner in his sinful deeds to which the second point refers.

6. *What, then, is the teaching of the second point?*

That there is an inwardly restraining operation of the Holy Spirit upon the heart of the natural man, which is not regenerating, whereby the progress of the corruption of sin in the human nature is being checked and restrained in such a way that a remnant of the original goodness in the state of righteousness is constantly preserved in it and also brought to bear fruit in many good works in this present life.

7. *What is the first element in this teaching?*

That there is in the sinner a remnant of natural good.

8. Why do you speak of "natural" good?

Because the defenders of the theory of common grace, one of the principal tenets of which is adopted in this second point, always emphasize the distinction between "natural" and "spiritual" good.

9. What is the difference?

The only conceivable difference is that by "spiritual" good is meant the good that is wrought in the depraved nature by the Spirit of Christ and is, therefore, rooted in regeneration; while by "natural" good is meant a good that is not so wrought by regenerating grace, but remains in man since the fall, and is, therefore, a remnant of his original goodness or righteousness.

10. What is implied in this "natural good" that remains in man since the fall, according to the exponents of this theory?

This "natural good," left to man after the fall, includes such important elements as a seed of external righteousness; receptivity for moral persuasion; receptivity for the truth; a will that is susceptible to good motives; and a conscience that is receptive for good influences, good inclinations, and desires of which the Holy Spirit can make use in restraining sin.

11. But how can you prove that this is actually implied in the teaching of the second point?

This is evident, not only from the language of this declaration itself, for it speaks, not of outward restraint, but of a general operation of the Holy Spirit; but it is also the explanation which is offered of the second point by one of its originators, Professor L. Berkhof, in his pamphlet on the Three Points.

12. But how is it explained that this remnant of "natural good" remained in man after his fall in Paradise?

Synod offered no explanation, neither do the exponents of the Three Points venture an explanation. The answer is, however, given by the chief exponent of the theory of common grace, Dr. A. Kuyper, Sr. He explains that common grace operated immediately after the fall of man, restraining and checking the corrupting power of sin. If there had not been such an immediate restraining operation of common grace upon the nature of man, he would have become utterly corrupt there and then. Man would have changed into a devil, and the development of mankind would have become an utter impossibility. But the restraining power of the Holy Spirit operated upon man as soon as he had sinned, so that he did not fully die, did not become all darkness, was not wholly corrupted, but retained some light and life, a remnant of his original goodness. And this remnant of good is preserved in mankind throughout its development in history.

13. What is the second element in the teaching of the second point?

The second element implied in the theory of the second point is this operation of the Holy Spirit, whereby the original good that remains in man since the fall is continuously guarded against further corruption, by checking and restraining the progress of sin. The remnant of original good that is left in man is the capital with which the Holy Spirit works. It is the treasure that must be preserved. Were there no good left in the natural man after the fall, there could be no further restraint. The corrupting process of the power of sin in man's nature would then have been completed. However, even this remnant of good in man would have become corrupted long ago if there had not been a constantly restraining operation of grace in the heart of man, which is not regenerating but preserving in nature. This constant operation of the Spirit, restraining the progress of sin, is the second element in the theory of common grace as embodied in the second point.

14. And what is the third element in this declaration of synod?

According to the explanation of Professor Berkhof, the second point also teaches an operation of the Holy Spirit, by which this remnant of natural good in the sinner becomes active. The seed of external righteousness germinates and brings forth fruit, so that the natural man performs good works in the sphere of natural and civil life.

15. What is the practical result of this restraining operation of the Holy Spirit?

That the natural man, who is supposedly dead in sin and misery, wholly corrupt and totally depraved, is able to live a naturally good, a morally sound life in this world. He is not regenerated. He is not ingrafted into Christ by a true and living faith. He therefore performs no spiritual good. But, by virtue of the remnant of good that is in him and the constant operation of the Holy Spirit upon him, the natural man really lives a weakened form of his original Paradise-life. He can perform good works in this world. To a certain extent he lives a good world-life.

16. What is one of the fundamental errors of this entire presentation of the truth?

That it conceives dualistically of sin in relation to God and implies a denial of the absolute sovereignty of the Most High even over the powers of sin and death. For, evidently, it presents sin and death as powers next to God and operating quite independently of Him. They are able of themselves, by some inherent principle, to work corruption in the heart and nature of man. But God checks this power. He therefore restrains a power that operates independently of Him. This is dualism. Scripture, however, gives us a radically different conception. Sin and death are not powers that work independently of God, but they are the result of His own cursing wrath against the sinner. They are but the executors of His righteous judgment and do that which is according to His good pleasure. And, conceiving of it thus, one cannot speak of a restraint of sin by God. The theory is rooted in a fundamentally dualistic conception and is a denial of the absolute sovereignty of God.

17. What other error is involved in the theory of the restraint of sin?

It impugns the righteousness of God and His justice with respect to the sinner. Death, including spiritual death, which involves total depravity, is the just punishment for sin. Thus God had threatened before the fall: "The day that thou eatest thereof, thou shalt surely die." Now, the exponents of the doctrine of the restraint of sin maintain that God did not fulfill this threat immediately after the fall. On the contrary, He graciously intervened and prevented death from wholly corrupting man.

But the question arises: On what ground of justice did God show this grace and cause it to operate? The defenders of this theory are wont to explain that grace is always unmerited favor, and this holds true of common grace. But they forget that the grace God manifests to His people in Christ is based on the atonement and perfect obedience of the Savior. Because of His righteousness they are righteous, and they receive all the blessings of grace as righteous in Him. But the world outside of Christ is without any such ground of righteousness on which it can justly be partaker of the grace of God. The theory, therefore, is an impugning of the righteousness of God.

18. Is there not still another error implied in the teaching of this second point?

There is. It is very clear that the entire theory of the restraint of sin is based on the error of resistible grace. The operation of the Holy Spirit, whereby the process of corruption in the heart of the sinner and in the world in general is held in check, is not irresistible. If it were, there would be no development of sin at all. But it is an undeniable fact, which is also plainly revealed in Scripture, that sin and corruption do continuously develop and increase in the world until the measure of iniquity is full and the man of sin can appear.

Now, if you inquire of the exponents of the theory of common grace how they account for this development of sin and corruption in the world, they reply that this is due to the fact that the Holy Spirit releases His restraining hold upon the sinner and gives him over in unrighteousness. And if you inquire further how it must be explained that the Spirit withdraws His restraining power of common grace from the sinner, the answer is, that the sinner resists this restraining influence of grace and thus goes from bad to worse. This, therefore, is the error of resistible grace. The power of the Spirit in this case is not efficacious. Man is stronger than God! This is an evident deviation from the truth of Scripture and our Reformed confessions.

19. But what is the principal objection against the second point and its implication?

That it is Pelagian.

20. Why is it Pelagian?

Because it is a very evident denial of the total depravity of the natural man.

21. Do the exponents of this theory admit this?

No, they deny this. They profess to maintain the Reformed truth of the total depravity of the natural man. They would even maintain that the truth of total depravity is presupposed in the teaching of the second point. And the very bold among them allege that only in the light of the theory of the restraint of sin by God's common grace is the doctrine of total depravity intelligible and tenable.

22. How do they go about to maintain this position?
They proceed from the supposition that the natural man still does many good works. For this position they do not appeal to Scripture, but to actual experience. Anyone can ascertain the fact of the good works of the natural man for himself. He lives a good world-life in many respects. It is even alleged that he often puts the Christian to shame. This being assumed, the question arises how this good the sinner does must be explained. Where is its fountain? Whence does it spring? From himself? In that case, they claim, you deny total depravity. And, therefore, you must explain the good works of the natural man from an operation of the Holy Spirit upon him, whereby the power of corruption in him is checked.

23. Do you, then, still maintain that the second point is Pelagian?
I do most emphatically.

24. Why do you?
Because, in this the theory agrees with Pelagianism, that in the fall man did not become wholly corrupt. Some remnant of his original goodness remained in him. True, there are a few points of difference between the fundamental tenet of the second point and Pelagianism. The latter attributes the goodness of the natural man to the character of the fall itself, the former to an operation of the Holy Spirit. The latter maintains that by this remnant of

his original goodness man can attain to the possession and performance of spiritual good, the former does not. But this does not alter the fact that both maintain that the natural man is not wholly corrupt and totally depraved. Fact is, that according to this theory there never was a totally depraved man in the world since the fall of our first parents. For, from the moment of the fall till the present day, there is the operation of this restraining grace in the heart of man, preserving in him the remnant of his original goodness, according to which he is able to live a tolerably good life in this world.

25. How would you characterize the teaching of the second point?

I would characterize the second point, with its theory of the restraint of sin, as a purely philosophic invention to apologize for the severity of the doctrine of total depravity and to compromise with the world.

26. What do you maintain to be the truth of the Word of God on this point?

That the natural man, ever since the fall of our first parents in Paradise, is wholly darkness and foolishness, corrupt before God in all his way, incapable of doing anything that is pleasing to Him, always inclined only to evil, until he is regenerated by the Spirit of Christ.

27. But were no gifts to him left after the fall?

Certainly, there is in him a remnant of natural light. He remained a rational moral being, endowed with reason and will, able to distinguish between good and evil. But there is nothing left in him of that light and knowledge according to which he may know that which is good and love it, nothing of righteousness and holiness, nothing of his original moral integrity. From the moment of the fall he became wholly corrupt. His knowledge of God changed into darkness, his righteousness into unrighteousness, his holiness into corruption. In Paradise his nature became exactly as corrupt as it could become.

28. Do you, then, deny that there is development of sin in the world?

Not at all. But we maintain that the manifestation of this corruption of the human nature in the actual sins of the race keeps pace with the organic development of the human race and follows this development. Adam's sin was a root-sin, which bears its fruit in all the actual sins of the entire race until the measure of iniquity is filled. As the race develops, and life with its many and various relationships becomes more complex, sin also reveals itself as corrupting the whole of life in all its relations. But upon this organic development there is no restraint. It proceeds exactly as fast as possible.

29. But is not this progress of sin controlled and limited by many factors?

It most certainly is. There is the all-overruling power of God, who indeed gives men over unto unrighteousness, and in His righteous judgment punishes sin with sin; but who also controls the progress of sin and leads it into those channels which are conducive to the realization of His counsel. There is the limitation imposed upon every man by the measure of his gifts, powers, and talents, by time and occasion, by means and circumstances, by character and disposition. All men do not commit all sin; each one sins according to his place in the organism of the race and in history. It is determined and limited by various and often conflicting motives, such as fear and shame, ambition and vain-glory, natural love and carnal lusts, malice and envy, hatred and vengeance. And it is influenced by the power of the magistrates. But in all these channels and under all these controlling and determining factors, many and various though they be, the current of sin and corruption moves onward without restraint and interruption, until it shall have served God's purpose and the measure of iniquity shall be filled!

Synod's Proof for the Second Point

1. Did the synod of 1924 prove that the theory of the restraint of sin through an operation of the Holy Spirit is confessionally Reformed?

It referred to two different passages of the Belgic Confession, which, however, teach something radically different from the contents of the second point.

2. Which are those passages?

The Belgic Confession, Articles 13 and 36.

3. How does Article 13 read in full?

As follows:

"We believe that the same God, after he had created all things, did not forsake them, or give them up to fortune or chance, but that he rules and governs them according to his holy will, so that nothing happens in this world without his appointment; nevertheless, God neither is the author of, nor can be charged with, the sins which are committed. For, his power and goodness are so great and incomprehensible, that he orders and executes his work in the most excellent and just manner, even then, when devils and wicked men act unjustly. And, as to what he doth surpassing human understanding, we will not curiously inquire into, farther than our capacity will admit of; but with the greatest humility and reverence adore the righteous judgments of God, which are hid from us, contenting ourselves that we are disciples of Christ, to learn only those things which he has revealed to us in his Word, without transgressing these limits. This doctrine affords us unspeakable consolation, since we are taught thereby that nothing can befall us by chance, but by the direction of our most gracious and heavenly Father; who watches over us with a paternal care, keeping all creatures so under his power, that not a hair of our head (for they are all numbered), nor a sparrow can fall to the ground, without the will of our Father, in whom we do entirely trust; being persuaded that he so restrains the devil and all our enemies, that without his will and permission, they cannot hurt us. And therefore we reject that damnable error of the Epicureans, who say that God regards nothing, but leaves all things to chance."

4. Is there any point of doctrine expressed in this article to which the Protestant Reformed Churches cannot subscribe?

Not at all. On the contrary, while these do and always did emphasize the truth as it is expressed in Article 13, the Christian Reformed Church is very weak on this point and always accuses those who do maintain it, that they make God the author of sin.

5. How, then, is it possible that they refer to this article as proof of the second point, and with an appeal to it cast out their Protestant Reformed brethren?

This is possible only because in the second point they "interpreted" this article to mean something radically different from what it actually teaches.

6. How can you prove that the alleged interpretation entirely distorts the meaning of the article?

First of all by pointing out that the second point of 1924 and Article 13 of the Belgic Confession deal with two different subjects. The former treats of general grace, the latter of divine providence. As is usually done by the exponents of the theory of common grace, synod confused grace and providence. What is merely God's omnipresent *power*, synod presents as God's omnipresent *grace*.

7. Have you more evidence that the meaning of Article 13 was wholly distorted in the second point of 1924?

Yes; synod speaks of a restraint of *sin through an influence of the Holy Spirit,* whereby some good is preserved in the natural man, so that he can live a naturally good life in this world; but the article speaks of a restraint of the *wicked* (the devil and all our enemies) by *keeping them under His power.* The difference is glaringly evident, so glaringly that it is difficult to suppose that the committee that composed the second point and the synod that adopted it were blinded by so great a stupidity that they could not detect it. The restraint of which the second point speaks is a spiritual, internal operation of God in the heart of the wicked, by virtue of which they somewhat improve their lives; but the article of the Belgic Confession speaks of an external compulsion, leaving the wicked morally unchanged, but bridling their wicked designs and leading them in those channels which may serve the purpose of the Almighty.

8. What especially should have prevented synod from quoting this article in proof of the statement that there is an operation of the Holy Spirit upon the heart of the wicked, checking the process of sin within him?

The fact that Article 13 includes the devil. God restrains the devil and all our enemies. By quoting the article in proof of the second point, synod actually adopted the doctrine that there is an operation of common grace through the Holy Spirit upon the devil, whereby he is not as wicked as he might be!

9. *How does Article 36 of the Belgic Confession read in full?*

It reads as follows:

"We believe that our gracious God, because of the depravity of mankind, hath appointed kings, princes and magistrates, willing that the world should be governed by certain laws and policies [i.e., police or police-regulations; French: *polices];* to the end that the dissoluteness of men might be restrained, and all things carried on among them with good order and decency. For this purpose he hath invested the magistracy with the sword, for the punishment of evil-doers and for the protection of them that do well. And their office is, not only to have regard unto, and watch for the welfare of the civil state; but also that they protect the sacred ministry; and thus may remove and prevent all idolatry and false worship; that the kingdom of antichrist may thus be destroyed and the kingdom of Christ promoted. They must therefore countenance the preaching of the Word of the gospel everywhere, that God may be honored and worshiped by everyone, as he commands in his Word. Moreover it is the bounden duty of every one, of what state, quality, or condition soever he may be, to subject himself to the magistrates; to pay tribute, to show due honor and respect to them, and to obey them in all things which are not repugnant to the Word of God; to supplicate for them in their prayers, that God may rule and guide them in all their ways, and that we may lead a quiet and peaceable life in all godliness and honesty. Wherefore we detest the Anabaptists and other seditious people, and in general all those who reject the higher powers and magistrates, and would subvert justice, introduce community of goods, and confound that decency and good order, which God hath established among men."

10. *What is described in this article?*

The calling of the magistrates according to the Word of God. What we have in this article is, evidently, the picture of a Christian government, according to the conception of our fathers. When the government functions according to its calling, it punishes the evil-doers and protects them that do well; it destroys the kingdom of antichrist and promotes the kingdom of Christ; and it furthers the preaching of the Word, so that God may be worshiped everywhere. And although the phrase "and thus may remove and prevent all idolatry and false worship" has been amended in a footnote, rejecting the dominion of the state over the church, yet the article as a whole was never repudiated.

11. But is there in this article any proof for the contention that there is an operation of the Holy Spirit restraining sin in the heart of the natural man?

Not at all. The difference between this article and the second point of 1924 is very lucid. Once more this article speaks of an external restraint upon and punishment of the wicked, and that not by God, but by the power of the magistrates and of their sword. So little does this part of the confession speak of a restraint of sin in the heart by the Holy Spirit, that if the latter were true the magistrates and the police would not be necessary for this purpose. It is exactly because of the dissoluteness of men, which is not restrained by any spiritual or moral improvement, that the government must bear the sword.

12. But do not the scriptural passages to which synod refers prove the truth of the second point?

Not at all; if synod had taken the trouble to interpret these references, it would undoubtedly have refrained from quoting them.

13. Which is the first passage to which synod refers?

Genesis 6:3: "And the LORD said, My spirit shall not always strive with man."

14. How would synod read this text?

Synod read this passage as follows: "And the LORD said: My Spirit shall not always restrain sin in the heart of man so as to improve him."

15. Why is this interpretation wholly impossible?

Because it would presuppose that, until that moment, the Spirit had actually restrained the process of sin in the heart of the wicked world, while the facts plainly contradict such a view. Wickedness in the pre-deluvian world had abounded and developed with astounding rapidity, so that, after sixteen centuries of development, the world was ripe for judgment, and its measure of iniquity was full. It is evident, therefore, that there had been no checking of the process and progress of sin in the world. This leaves only two possibilities: either the Spirit of God had attempted to stem the tide of sin, but had utterly failed, which is blasphemy even to think; or there had been no such operation of the Spirit of God upon the heart of man as synod declares to be taught in this text. The latter is the truth.

16. Does not the context also contradict the interpretation of synod?

It does, for in verse 5 we read: "And God saw that the wickedness of man was great in the earth, and that every imagination of the thoughts of his heart was only evil continually." It is quite impossible that, given an operation of the Holy Spirit upon that heart of man, every imagination arising from it could be only and continually evil.

17. What, then, is the meaning of Genesis 6:3?

"Strive" in the text has the meaning of striving or opposing by the Word. It is evident from Scripture that the Holy Spirit had striven with the wicked world before the flood through the Word of God by the pre-deluvian patriarchs. Thus we read in Jude 14, 15: "And Enoch also, the seventh from Adam, prophesied of these, saying, Behold, the Lord cometh with ten thousands of his saints, to execute judgment upon all, and to convince all that are ungodly among them of all their ungodly deeds which they have ungodly committed, and of all their hard speeches which ungodly sinners have spoken against him."

From this passage it is evident that the Spirit did strive with the ungodly world, not by an operation of the Holy Spirit upon the hearts of the ungodly, but by the Word of the prophets. It is also plain from this text that the ungodly sinners contradicted the Word of God and spoke "hard speeches" against it. And thus it is easily to be understood that over against this striving of the Spirit the world increased in sin. The Word of God, as always, had a hardening effect. And this interpretation, while it is in harmony with the text itself, is also in accord with the general teaching of the Word of God, that the Word is a savor of death unto death for the ungodly and that it hardens men's hearts if by it they are not converted to God.

18. Which other passages does synod quote in proof of the second point?

It refers to five different texts that speak of a "giving over" of the ungodly by an act of God.

19. Which are these five texts?

They are the following:

Psalm 81:11, 12: "But my people would not hearken to my voice; and Israel would none of me. So I gave them up unto their own hearts' lusts: and they walked in their own counsels."

Acts 7:42: "Then God turned, and gave them up to worship the host of heaven; as it is written in the book of the prophets, O ye house of Israel, have ye offered to me slain beasts and sacrifices by the space of forty years in the wilderness?"

Romans 1:24: "Wherefore God also gave them up to uncleanness through the lusts of their own hearts, to dishonour their own bodies between themselves."

Romans 1:26: "For this cause God gave them up unto vile affections: for even their women did change the natural use into that which is against nature."

Romans 1:28: "And even as they did not like to retain God in their knowledge, God gave them over to a reprobate mind, to do those things which are not convenient."

20. Do these passages teach what the synod elicited from them?

Even a cursory reading ought to be sufficient to convince one that the very opposite from a restraint of sin is taught in all these passages. It must be clear to all who can read that "to give up" is the very opposite of restraint.

21. But how could synod quote passages that are so evidently in contradiction with its own declaration in the second point?

It understands the phrase "God gave them up" or "He gave them over" in the sense of "ceasing from restraining them any longer." Thus synod would read all these passages as if they merely signified that whereas God formerly restrained the mad course of the ungodly, He now let them go and allowed them to run their own way to destruction. In this way do they arrive at the conclusion that, although these passages do not directly speak of a restraint of sin, they do presuppose such a restraint on the part of God as preceding the moment of the giving up.

22. Is this interpretation tenable?

No, for, in the first place, it does not allow the full significance to the term "to give up" or "to give over." The word used in the original in the passages quoted by synod is frequently employed in Scripture and always refers to a positive act of delivering up. Thus the word is used in all the four gospel narratives to denote the act of Pilate whereby he delivered up Jesus to be crucified, where the word certainly cannot signify the same as "to let go." And in this sense it is used in many other places, while it never has the meaning which the synod would ascribe to it in the passages quoted. Hence, the interpretation of synod distorts the true meaning of Scripture in these passages.

23. Is there not another reason why the interpretation of synod is untenable?

Yes, the reason, namely, that no such restraint of sin can possibly be presupposed as preceding the moment of the "giving up" in any of the passages quoted. The very opposite is true. In Psalm 81:11, 12 and Acts 7:42 the reference is to wicked Israel, to whom God had sent His Word by Moses and the prophets, but who had constantly revealed that they would not hearken to the voice of the Lord. They had not been restrained by an operation of common grace, but, on the contrary, they were hardened in sin. Sin had taken its course and, over against the Word of God, they had hardened their hearts. It was then that the Lord turned to give them up to worship all the host of heaven. The giving up, therefore, is a positive act of God as a punishment for their sin in which they had developed and increased.

Still more clearly evident this is in the passages which synod quoted from the first chapter of the epistle to the

Romans. In verses 18-23 the apostle certainly does not describe a restraining influence of the Holy Spirit upon the wicked heathen world, whereby the heathen had lived a morally good life in this world, but on the contrary he speaks of a manifestation of the wrath of God from heaven all through the ages of history, from the very beginning of the world's sinful course, against all ungodliness and unrighteousness of men, who hold the truth in ungodliness.

Instead of common grace, therefore, there is wrath revealed from heaven. And instead of a tolerably good life as a fruit of the operation of the Holy Spirit, there is found in men a holding of the truth in unrighteousness. They knew God, but they glorified Him not as God, neither were thankful. And what was God's attitude over against this ungodliness of wicked men? Did He restrain them? Did He cause a gracious operation of the Holy Spirit to work in their hearts, so that they would not corrupt themselves? The very opposite is taught in the passages which synod quotes. He gave them over. He made them foolish, so that they worshiped men and beasts and creeping things. And not only did He deliver them up to religious folly and darkness, but He also gave them up to moral uncleanness and corruption, to vile affections, to a reprobate mind, to do things which are not convenient.

Except for the fact, then, that the synodical committee that composed the Three Points and the synod after them blindly followed Dr. A. Kuyper, Sr. in the use and application he makes of these passages, it may be considered inexplicable that these passages were at all adduced in support of the second point. They teach the very opposite from that which synod attempted to set forth.

24. Did not synod refer to still another text to establish the second point?

Indeed; it also referred to II Thessalonians 2:6, 7: "And now ye know what withholdeth that he might be revealed in his time. For the mystery of iniquity doth already work; only he who now letteth will let, until he be taken out of the way."

25. What is the implied contention of synod with respect to this passage from Scripture?

That "what withholdeth" is the power of common grace; and "he who now letteth and will let" is the Holy Spirit. Hence, the conclusion is that the development of the power of antichrist to which the text refers is restrained by the power of common grace and the influence of the Holy Spirit in the hearts of sinful men.

26. What may be said of this interpretation?

That it is extremely arbitrary and farfetched, to say the least. Certain it is that the text does not speak of common grace as the withholding power, nor as the Holy Spirit as the One who now letteth and will let. At the very best, the interpretation is a mere conjecture and invention of ingenious minds. Besides, it presupposes that the Thessalonians had already become acquainted with the doctrine of common grace; we conjecture it must also be supposed that the apostle had taken pains to instruct them in this wonderful theory. For, he writes to them: "And now *ye know* what withholdeth."

27. But is this interpretation not probably correct?

On the contrary, this explanation or conjecture is probably very incorrect. For, first of all, it is very improbable that the Thessalonians knew that it was the power of common grace that was withholding the man of sin. How strange it would be that the apostle should presuppose knowledge on the part of the Thessalonians of a doctrine of which he himself never writes in his epistles! In the second place, it is entirely safe to say that, if the apostle had meant to refer to the Holy Spirit in this passage, he would have mentioned Him by name, for he always does. He would certainly not have expressed himself so cryptically, that all might have their guess as to what he really meant. And in the third place, Scripture would not write of the Holy Spirit: "until he be taken out of the way." For all these reasons the conjecture of synod is very improbable, if not quite impossible.

28. What is a far more plausible interpretation of this text?

That the apostle is referring to a definite power and person, known to the Thessalonians, that in those days stood in the way of the full realization of the anti-Christian kingdom. We know not what person and what power the apostle had in mind, neither need we know. Every attempt to determine this must needs be mere conjecture. But this power and person certainly is a type of all those historical powers and persons and circumstances that prevent the ultimate manifestation of the kingdom of antichrist before God's own time.

29. Did synod offer still more proof from Scripture?

No; we examined all the evidence synod adduced.

30. May it, then, be maintained that synod clearly established the second point as being scriptural and confessionally Reformed?

On the contrary, everyone will have to admit that it miserably failed in this respect.

The Third Point
and Its Implications

1. Will you literally quote again the third point of doctrine adopted by the Christian Reformed Church in 1924?

Yes, it reads as follows:

"Relative to the third point, which is concerned with the question of civil righteousness as performed by the unregenerate, synod declares that according to Scripture and the Confessions the unregenerate, though incapable of doing any saving good, can do civil good. This is evident from Dordrecht, III/IV, 4, and from the Netherlands Confession, Article 36, which teach that God without renewing the heart so influences man that he is able to perform civil good; while it also appears from the citations from Reformed writers of the most flourishing period of Reformed theology, that our Reformed fathers from ancient times were of the same opinion."

2. Which are the passages from the confessions to which synod refers in support of this declaration?

They are:

Canons III/IV, 4: "There remain, however, in man since the fall, the glimmerings of natural light, whereby he retains some knowledge of God, of natural things, and of the differences between good and evil, and discovers some regard for virtue, good order in society, and for maintaining an orderly external deportment."

Belgic Confession, Article 36: "Wherefore we detest ... all those who ... confound that decency and good order, which God hath established among men."

3. What is the relation between the second and the third point?

The relation between the doctrines declared by the second and the third point is like that of cause and effect. Both declarations speak of an operation for good upon the natural man which is not regenerative. The second point teaches that by this operation of the Holy Spirit the natural man is somewhat improved, so that he is not so depraved as without this operation he would be; the third point refers to the fruit of this operation of God upon the natural man, consisting in his power to do civil good.

4. What is briefly the teaching of the third point?

That, by virtue of a positive influence of God upon him for good, the unregenerate is able to do good works in the sphere of things natural and civil.

5. Does not the third point state that the natural man is unable to do any saving good?

It does, indeed.

6. What did synod of 1924 mean by the distinction between saving or spiritual and civil or natural good?

It may justly be doubted if the synod had any clear distinction in mind. However, judging from its declarations and from later interpretations of these three points of doctrine by some leaders of the Christian Reformed Church, synod understood this distinction as follows:

   a. Both spiritual and natural good are good in a moral sense before God. Neither of them may be called sin.

b. Spiritual good has its source in the regenerating influence of the Spirit of Christ; natural good in the unregenerated nature of the sinner as restrained and preserved from total corruption by the influence of the Spirit of God.

c. Saving good is eternal and consists in conversion, sanctification, and perseverance unto the end; civil good is temporal and has reference to and value for the things and sphere of this present life only.

7. Is it not true that synod also had in mind the distinction between outward and inward good?

No, this cannot be maintained. Synod certainly intended to say and did clearly express that civil righteousness, or the natural good of the unregenerate man, is good inwardly, that is, proceeds from his mind and will. This is evident from the fact that the synod spoke of an operation of the Holy Spirit and of an influence of God upon the sinner, and such operations are always inward. And this is plain, too, from the interpretation Christian Reformed leaders have offered of this third point. Professor L. Berkhof, for instance, wrote on this point as follows: "His works may be called good, in a subjective sense, in as far as they are the fruit of inclinations and affections touching the mutual relations of men, which are themselves relatively good, are still operating in man; and in an objective sense, if they in regard to the matter as such are works prescribed by the law, and in the sphere of social life correspond to a purpose that is well-pleasing to God" (The Three Points, pp. 50, 51).

8. From what else is it evident that synod actually intended to declare that the natural man is capable of performing what is positively good?

From its condemnation of the views of the Reverends

H. Danhof and H. Hoeksema, which had been published before the synod in 1924 and in opposition to which the second and third points were formulated. They had written on this matter as follows:

"And what, then, is civil righteousness? According to our view, the natural man discerns the relationships, laws, rules of life and fellowship, etc., as they are ordained by God. He sees their propriety and utility. And he adapts himself to them for his own sake. If in this attempt he succeeds the result is an act that shows an outward and formal resemblance to the laws of God. Then we have civil righteousness, a regard for virtue and external deportment. And if in this attempt he fails, as is frequently the case, civil righteousness disappears, and the result is exactly the opposite. His fundamental error, however, is that he does not seek after God, nor aim at Him and His glory, even in this regard for virtue and external deportment. On the contrary he seeks himself, both individually and in fellowship with other sinners and with the whole world, and it is his purpose to maintain himself even in his sin over against God. And this is sin. And in reality his work also has evil effects upon himself and his fellow creatures. For, his actions with relation to men and his fellow creatures are performed according to the same rule and with similar results. And thus it happens that sin develops constantly and corruption increases, while still there remains a formal adaptation to the laws ordained of God for the present life. Yet, the natural man never attains to any ethical good. That is our view" (*Along Straight Paths*, pp. 72, 73).

9. What are the implications of the third point?
The first implication is a separation of the spiritual and moral or the spiritual and natural, a separation of the first and second tables of the law of God.

10. Why do you say that such a separation is implied in the third point?

Because the third point plainly declares that the natural man is incapable of doing saving or spiritual good, while he is nevertheless able to perform what is good in the spheres of this present life. According to synod and the leaders in the Christian Reformed Church, the same act may be spiritually corrupt and worthy of eternal damnation, and morally good and pleasing to the Lord. An act may not be rooted in and proceed from faith, yet it may be good.

11. What is another implication in this third point?

The second implication of the third point is that there is conflict between the doctrine of total depravity and the actual working out and application of this truth.

12. How could you make this clear?

It is the official confession of the Christian Reformed Church that the natural man is incapable of doing any good and inclined to all evil. Moreover, it is their confession that only those are good works that proceed from a true faith, are done according to the law of God and to His glory, and not those that are based upon our imagination or on the institutions of men. Yet, although in the abstract and as a matter of their confession the Christian Reformed Church admits this, in practical life it professes it to be wholly different. In this life, with respect to the things and spheres of this world, there is nowhere a totally depraved man, according to them. All are able to do good. All can live a morally good life. They condemn it in the strongest terms as absolutism, when one maintains the confessions and applies it to real men in the real world. Total depravity has become a mere abstraction in the Christian Reformed Church.

13. What is a third implication in the third point?

The third implication is that a man can do good works, which are, nevertheless, not to be accounted as his own, and for which he can expect no reward. This is emphasized repeatedly by the exponents of the theory of common grace, and by defenders of the Three Points. The good works of the natural man are really not his, no more than it is to be attributed to a boat that the steersman forces it in a direction opposite from that in which the wind would naturally blow it. "If man were left to himself," writes Professor Berkhof, "he would not be able to perform even this civil good.... For this reason this natural good does not entitle man to any claim of reward" (*The Three Points,* p. 52).

14. What is the fourth implication in the third point?

That properly the good work of the natural man is the good work of the Holy Spirit without its being the work of the natural man at all. The Spirit of God so influences the corrupt nature of the unregenerated man, that in his case the evil tree brings forth good fruit. He does not penetrate to the heart of the natural man. The heart remains corrupt. In that heart is nothing but unrighteousness and enmity against God. Yet, God so influences the nature of the sinner, his thoughts and his will, his affections and desires, that with a heart full of hatred against God he performs that which is pleasing in the sight of God. The Spirit forces, compels the operations of that wicked nature to go in the right direction, even as the helmsman forces a vessel to sail against the wind. It may be impossible to conceive of so monstrous a thing, but it is emphatically the teaching of the third point.

15. What is the practical application and result of the doctrine upheld in the third point?

The result is that in practical life the official teaching

of the church that man is totally depraved and is incapable of doing any good, while inclined to all evil, is forgotten. The world that is professed to be in darkness is magically flooded with light by the wonder of common grace. Nowhere do you find the corrupt man as described in the Heidelberg Catechism, Lord's Day III, and in the Canons of Dordrecht, III/IV, 1-4. Practically, the difference between the righteous and the unrighteous is wiped out. It is even alleged that the latter put the former to shame! The theoretically depraved are actually wonderfully good! There is a good deal of harmony between righteousness and unrighteousness. Much concord is established between Christ and Belial!

16. Which are your general and principal objections against the teaching of the third point?

First of all, it may be objected against this declaration that it lowers the standard of moral, ethical good, and thus necessarily obliterates the distinction between good and evil, righteousness and unrighteousness, light and darkness. The definition of good works, which the Heidelberg Catechism gives, that they are those that proceed from a true faith, are done according to the law of God and to His glory, certainly does not hold for the "good" of which the third point speaks. There is another good, that is neither good nor evil, or rather, that is both. The exponents of the Three Points speak of the relativity of good and evil. Professor Berkhof speaks of a good that is relatively sinful and of sin that is relatively good. He speaks of the good in the full sense of the word, and of "what is truly good," and implies that there is also a good that is not truly good, not good in the full sense.

And he condemns as absolutism the view that the natural man can only sin and does sin at all times. This notion of relativity with respect to the sphere of ethics and morality is pernicious. For it creates a sphere of transition, a domain where righteousness and unrighteousness, Christ and Belial may have fellowship and live the same life. Of the practical results of the preaching and teaching of such a doctrine one fears even to think. For while the leaders, at least some of them, may be able for a time to maintain the dualistic position that the natural man is totally depraved, yet that he is not, and that the world is corrupt and in darkness, yet that it is flooded with light and manifests much goodness, those whom they instruct will not maintain that position. And they will be swallowed up by the world.

17. Have you any other objection against the teaching of the third point?

Yes; it also must be objected that it implies an impugning of the holiness of God. For, the so-called good that is performed by the ungodly is directly ascribed to the operation of the Holy Spirit and to the influence of God upon the sinner. What is admittedly a very imperfect good, a sinful good, a relative good, the withered fruit of an uprooted tree; what is in actual fact very corrupt and evil, is presented as the fruit of an operation of the Holy Spirit. It is the Spirit who adorns the corrupt tree with good fruit, causes it to appear like a good tree and thus, according to the theory of common grace, creates what is virtually a lie! For it is declared that man himself is incapable of bringing forth these good fruits. He is dead in trespasses and sins. He is like a tree cut off from its roots. But the Spirit causes that dead tree to yield good fruit without making the tree alive!

These fruits, then, are not rooted in the love of God, they do not at all proceed from faith; they are performed by or through a man that stands in enmity against God. And of such fruits the Spirit is alleged to be the author! Is it, then, not literally true, that the third point makes God the author of sin?

18. What other objection have you?

The teaching of the third point is that of moral determinism, and it destroys the freedom of man as a moral agent. According to the presentation of the third point and its interpretation by the leaders of the Christian Reformed Church, man is no moral agent at all in performing the good he does, and for that reason he can lay no claim to any reward. Remember that by this influence of God or operation of the Holy Spirit the heart of man is not renewed. He is supposed to remain dead in trespasses and sins. As such he remains totally incapable of doing any good and inclined to all evil. Even his supposedly good works do not proceed from his own heart. His *ego* is not involved. If he were let alone, he would only do evil. The Spirit, then, compels man to do good works wholly contrary to the intents of his own heart. The result is that the Spirit is the real author of the works of man, while the latter is a mere tool. And thus the moral character of man is destroyed, his responsibility is denied, and a theory of moral determinism is presented as Reformed doctrine!

19. What other objection is closely connected with the former?

It must be objected against the third point, that it attacks the justice of God. God's justice is always manifest in this that He strictly rewards the good with good and He punishes the evil. But the third point would have us adopt the view that the natural man performs much good in this world for the which he is never rewarded. It is emphasized that the natural man performs good works in this life.

If we judge according to the standard of the third point, it ought not to be difficult to find many men in the world who hardly sin. They commit no gross iniquities; they live temperately and chastely; in their external deportment they are blameless; they even will sacrifice themselves for the well-being of humanity.

All this is called good in the sight of God. The Lord judges it to be good. It may not be called sin. Yet, when they have thus walked their whole life they are, according to this theory, cast into eternal perdition. All these good works that sinners do have no reward whatever.

It is evident, then, that the entire moral order is subverted, and that the justice of God is denied.

20. What, however, is your principal objection?
That the third point is Pelagian.

21. What do you mean by this?
I mean that, when one sets aside all sophistical arguments by which it is attempted to defend the third point and to show that it is in harmony with the Reformed view of the truth, it is nothing but a denial of the total depravity of the natural man. And this is the main error of the Pelagian theory.

22. Do the exponents of the theory of common grace and the defenders of this third point admit this?
On the contrary, they most strenuously deny this and maintain that it is the only possible standpoint upon which the truth of total depravity can be maintained. They claim that, as we look about in the world, it cannot be denied that the natural man performs many good works.

The doctrine of total depravity, therefore, does not seem to fit. How, then, can we maintain this doctrine and yet explain the good works of natural man? By denying that they proceed from himself, from his heart, and by teaching that these good works are really the work of the Holy Spirit!

23. What is the fundamental error of this reasoning?

That it does not let the Word of God, but the sinful judgment of man determine what is good and evil. As we shall see later, Scripture nowhere teaches that the works of the natural man are good, even though they would appear thus to our sinful judgment. But, in opposition to the plain teaching of Scripture, the reasoning implied in the third point proceeds from the error that sinners do much good.

24. What is the real teaching of the third point?

The third point teaches that man *would have been* and *would be* totally depraved, i.e, wholly incapable of doing any good and inclined to all evil, if there were no general operation of the Holy Spirit and influence of God upon him by which he is able to do good works. If there were no influence of common grace in the world, the natural man would be totally depraved. Now, however, he is not.

25. Are, then, the Three Points very dangerous errors?

They are, for they imply all the fundamental errors of Arminius and Pelagius. The first point is principally a denial that the grace of God is particular, since it teaches that the preaching of the gospel is grace to all that hear the gospel; the second and third points are fundamentally a denial of the scriptural doctrine of the total depravity of the natural man. And these errors are all the more dangerous because they pretend to be in conformity with the Reformed confessions. It is no exaggeration to maintain that they are the wolf in sheep's clothing, the devil presenting himself as an angel of light.

Synod's Proof
for the Third Point

1. Did the synod of 1924 claim to find proof for the implications of the third point in the confessions?

Indeed; it mentions the Canons of Dordrecht, III/IV, 4; and the Netherlands or Belgic Confession, Article 36.

2. What do you read in the Canons, III/IV, 4?

The entire article reads as follows:

"There remain, however, in man since the fall, the glimmerings of natural light, whereby he retains some knowledge of God, of natural things, and of the differences between good and evil, and discovers some regard for virtue, good order in society, and for maintaining an orderly external deportment. But so far is this light of nature from being sufficient to bring him to a saving knowledge of God, and to true conversion, that he is incapable of using it aright even in things natural and civil. Nay further, this light, such as it is, man in various ways renders wholly polluted, and holds it in unrighteousness, by doing which he becomes inexcusable before God."

3. Why do you emphasize that the entire article reads thus?

Because the committee synod had appointed to serve her with advice in this matter did not quote the article entirely, but only the first sentence of it.

4. Why would the committee have done so?

A superficial reading of the first sentence of this article might leave the impression upon the minds of the imprudent and inexperienced that it actually teaches that the natural man is able to do good works, as the third point would have us believe. However, as soon as the sentence is taken in its proper context and the entire article is considered, it becomes perfectly evident that this cannot possibly be the meaning. The last two sentences emphatically contradict what synod claims is taught in the first part of this article.

5. What does the first part of this article, the part which the committee quoted, teach?

a. That fallen man retained some glimmerings of natural light.

b. That by this natural light he has some knowledge of God, of things natural, and of the difference between good and evil.

c. That by this natural light he discovers some regard for virtue, for good order in society, and for maintaining an orderly external deportment.

6. What is "natural light"?

It is the light of reason, through which man, even after the fall, is a rational-moral being. The article speaks of "glimmerings" of this light remaining in fallen man, because it does no longer shine in the original brightness that characterized it in the state of righteousness. If man had not retained these glimmerings he would not be able to act rationally and morally in relation to God and man. He would not be responsible. He would be unable to sin; for sin presupposes a rational being that knows what he *ought* to do and is, therefore, responsible. And he could not be subject to punishment, nor would he be in a position to justify God in His righteous judgment. In the light of these glimmerings, therefore, fallen man *knows* what he *ought* to do, but is not morally able to do it. Knowledge is no virtue.

7. What knowledge of God does fallen man have in the light of these glimmerings?

He knows that God is and that He is One, eternal in power and divinity, and that He must be glorified and thanked. This knowledge, which by his glimmerings of natural light he is able to perceive, God shows unto him, for the invisible things of God from the creation of the world are clearly seen, being understood by the things that are made (Rom. 1:19, 20). By this knowledge, therefore, he knows what he *ought* to be and to do in relation to God *as God.* He must glorify and thank Him. However, the question as to whether there remains in fallen man any *good* and the ability to do good is not determined by what he *knows,* but by what, in the light of that knowledge, he *does.* And the Word of God teaches that, knowing God, he refuses to glorify Him as God and to be thankful (Rom. 1:21).

8. What is his knowledge of "natural things"?

Natural things are the things of this world, things earthy, man himself and creation about him, the different creatures in relation one to another and to himself. In the light of this knowledge man, fallen man, is able to live his present earthly life, such as it is. In this light he also develops the sciences and discovers the hidden powers of creation and invents the wonders of the modern world. He discovers numerous means whereby to enrich the life of the world. Again, however, the question as to whether there remains in fallen man any good, and whether he performs any good, is not answered by the fact that he is able to live and to enlarge upon the scope of his earthly

life, but is determined by his relation to God. With all
these means he does not improve, neither does he do any
good. He merely subjects himself with all these to the
service of sin.

9. But does not the article also state that he knows the difference between good and evil?

Indeed; and thus it is. Were it not so, man could not
be a sinner. However, it must be emphasized once more,
the question is not whether he *knows* the difference between good and evil, but whether, knowing this, he
performs the good. And this he does not do, will not do,
and cannot will to do.

10. Yet, does not the article also state that in the light of these glimmerings the natural man discovers some regard for virtue, for good order in society, and for maintaining an orderly external deportment?

Indeed; and we do not deny it. This means, in the first
place, that the fallen man, though he loves sin and hates
God, knows very well that God is good, and that it is also
good to serve Him. He is not unaware of the patent fact
that sin leads to destruction. Thus he also knows that the
law of God is good and that to keep that law in his earthly
life is good *for him.* He perceives very well that it is not
good *for him* to commit adultery, to steal, and to murder.
Hence, he has a certain regard for virtue, and there is even
a certain manifest attempt in his life and walk to be
virtuous, to maintain order in society, and to conduct
himself orderly in his external deportment.

But this regard and this attempt is only manifest in as
far as he perceives in certain cases that transgression of
the law in his actual and outward life has evil effects for
himself, and in as far as, induced by this fear of evil
results, he is able to control his lust. This explains also
why he succeeds, but to a very limited extent, in this

attempt to be virtuous. He is not always equally mindful of the evil effects of sin; nor, being mindful of it, does he always succeed in bridling his lust.

Hence, though there is some regard for virtue and good order and orderly external deportment, it must be remarked:

a.   That inwardly he is not virtuous at all, but even in this regard for virtue a seeker of self. He does not love God, neither God's precepts, but seeks to maintain himself.

b.   That outwardly he appears virtuous in a very limited extent, and, in spite of the attempt to keep within the bounds of safety, he and all the world are nevertheless dominated by sin and are rushing to destruction. The rule is that "knowing the judgment of God, that they which commit such things are worthy of death, not only do the same, but have pleasure in them that do them" (Rom. 1:32).

11. Is there, then, even in that first part of Canons III/IV, 4, which was quoted by the committee, no proof for the doctrinal contents of the third point?

Indeed not. The third point teaches that God, without renewing the heart, so influences man that he is able to do civil good. True, the natural light is a gift of God to man. But, as we have seen, mere knowledge is no virtue. And who would dare to call good that man who refuses to glorify and thank God in the glimmerings of that natural light? Or, who would stamp as good works those limited attempts of man to seek himself by keeping within the bounds of the law of God? And is it not little short of blasphemy to ascribe these corruptions to an influence of God and to the operations of the Holy Spirit? The interpretation which the synod of 1924 would put upon Canons III/IV, 4 must be considered as extremely corrupt.

12. But did you not say that the last part of this article of the Canons contradicts plainly what synod claimed to be taught in the first part?

Indeed, I did. And the truth of this statement must be evident to all who do not willingly close their eyes to what is very evident. For, while the first part of this article states the fact that the natural man retained some glimmerings of natural light, in the second part we are taught what he does with it. "But so far is this light of nature from being sufficient to bring him to a saving knowledge of God, and to true conversion, that he is incapable of using it aright even in things natural and civil. Nay further, this light, such as it is, man in various ways renders wholly polluted, and holds it in unrighteousness, by doing which he becomes inexcusable before God."

13. Does not this last part teach that with this natural light the fallen man is incapable of doing saving and spiritual good, and is this not admitted by the third point?

Indeed, this is taught in this article of the Canons. The Canons were written against the Arminians, who taught that the natural man could use these glimmerings of natural light unto spiritual improvement, so that he could advance by them to the greater light of a saving knowledge of God. It is for this reason that this article denies that the natural light is serviceable for the fallen man to bring him to such saving knowledge. On this point we have no controversy with synod and the third point. But what synod declared was that the unregenerate, though incapable of doing any saving good, can do civil good.

14. Why, then, do you maintain that the last part of this article of the Canons contradicts plainly what synod claims to be taught by the first part of the same?

Because in this last part the Canons teach far more than merely that the natural man by his natural light cannot attain to a saving knowledge of God.

15. What does it teach?

First of all, that fallen man is incapable of using the natural light aright in things natural and civil. Synod attempted to prove, by quoting only the first part, that he is capable of using this natural light aright in the sphere of things natural and civil, so that he can do civil good. And that synod really meant to declare that the natural man can do good works in the sphere of the natural and civil is evident from the fact that it ascribed this power to an influence of God and, in the light of the second point, to an operation of the Holy Spirit. This contention, then, is plainly contradicted in the last part of this article of the Canons.

16. What else does this last part teach?

It very emphatically maintains that fallen man renders this natural light wholly polluted in various ways, and that he holds it in unrighteousness. This can only mean that, though he knows the difference between good and evil in the sphere of things natural and civil, though he knows what he ought to be and to do, yet he sins and corrupts himself and all of life. When the natural man wholly pollutes and corrupts the natural light and holds it in unrighteousness, he certainly cannot be said to do civil good at the same time. Hence, the plain and emphatic language of the last part of this article contradicts the interpretation synod puts upon the first sentence.

17. What other part of the confession did synod quote to prove the truth of the third point?

The third point refers to Article 36 of the Belgic Confession, of which the committee quoted the following

fragment: "wherefore we detect ... all those who ...
confound that decency and good order, which God hath
established among men."

18. What would you answer to this?

I would say that synod must have been desperately
looking for anything that would have a semblance of
proof in the confessions, before it finally decided to
appear in public with this attempt.

19. Why do you say this?

Because in this quotation even the semblance of proof
for the truth of the third point is utterly wanting. It
certainly contains no proof for the contention that there is
an influence of God upon man, an operation of the Holy
Spirit which is not regenerative upon the sinner, by which
he is able to do civil good in the sight of God.

But this utter want of the desired and pretended proof
is rendered beyond all reasonable doubt as soon as we
complete the fragment synod quotes. For, thus completed, it reads as follows: "Wherefore, we detest the
Anabaptists and other seditious people, and in general all
those who reject the higher powers and magistrates, and
would subvert justice, introduce community of goods,
and confound that decency and good order which God
hath established among men." It will be evident that this
part of the confession does not at all speak of the good
fallen man can do, but of good order and decency God
establishes among men. The reference in this article is to
the government, by which God wills that the world shall
be ruled. That in the midst of this God-ordained order of
life and society the fallen man does not sin, yea, that he
does not even corrupt this very order and press it into the
service of sin, the article does not state.

On the contrary, if we apply to this article the last part
of the Canons III/IV, 4, it will be evident that our confes-

sions teach that, even in things natural and civil, hence also in things pertaining to governments and magistrates, fallen man wholly pollutes his natural light and holds it in unrighteousness. Both history and actual conditions of the present day amply corroborate this judgment.

20. Do not other parts of the confessions clearly oppose the declaration of synod in the third point?
Indeed, they do.

21. Will you quote some of them?
Yes; in answer to the question: "Are we then so corrupt that we are wholly incapable of doing any good and inclined to all evil?" the Heidelberg Catechism declares in Lord's Day III, Q. & A. 8: "Indeed we are; except we are regenerated by the Spirit of God."

22. Can you quote another passage?
Certainly. The same Catechism teaches in Lord's Day XXXIII, A. 91, that good works are "only those which proceed from a true faith, are performed according to the law of God, and to his glory; and not such as are founded on our imaginations, or the institutions of men." Now, synod admits that the good works of which it is speaking in the third point do not proceed from a regenerated heart; hence, they are not of faith. They are not done to the glory of God, nor are they in harmony with the law of God, the principle of which is the love of God. Hence, they certainly are not good works. They are, in fact, based on our own imaginations and on the institutions of men. And, as the Catechism emphasizes that *only* such as are described in answer 91 are good works, the third point plainly deviates from and contradicts the confession.

23. What does the Heidelberg Catechism have to say on this subject in Lord's Day XLIV, Q. & A. 114?

There it gives an answer to the question, whether the Christian can keep the commandments of God perfectly. And it asserts that this is impossible, but that, on the contrary, even the holiest men, while in this life, have but a small beginning of this obedience, yet so, that with a sincere resolution they begin to live, not only according to some, but all the commandments of God. How is it possible that this same Christian, who upon candid self-examination finds that he has but a small beginning of this obedience, should declare of the unregenerated man that he is able to do good works in the sphere of natural and civil life? Evidently the declaration of the third point is quite contrary to the spirit, as well as to the plain teaching of our confessions.

24. What do we confess in Article 14 of the Belgic Confession?

"We believe that God created man out of the dust of the earth, and made and formed him after his own image and likeness, good, righteous, and holy, capable in all things to will agreeably to the will of God. But being in honor, he understood it not, neither knew his excellency, but wilfully subjected himself to sin, and consequently to death, and the curse, giving ear to the words of the devil. For the commandment of life, which he had received, he transgressed; and by sin separated himself from God, who was his true life, having corrupted his whole nature; whereby he made himself liable to corporal and spiritual death. And being thus become wicked, perverse, and corrupt in all his ways, he hath lost all his excellent gifts, which he had received from God, and only retained a few remains thereof, which, however, are sufficient to leave man without excuse; for all the light which is in us is changed into darkness, as the Scriptures teach us, saying: The light shineth in darkness and the darkness comprehendeth it not; where St. John calleth men dark-ness."

No commentary is needed to show that there is in this article no room for any capability of doing good on the part of the natural man.   He is wicked, perverse, and corrupt *in all his ways,* that is, in all his actual life in the world!

25. Have you still more proof against the third point from the confessions?

The Canons of Dordrecht teach in III/IV, 1: "Man was originally formed after the image of God. His under-standing was adorned with a true and saving knowledge of his Creator, and of spiritual things; his heart and will were upright; all his affections pure; and the whole man was holy; but revolting from God by the instigation of the devil, and abusing the freedom of his own will, he for-feited these excellent gifts; and on the contrary entailed on himself blindness of mind, horrible darkness, vanity and perverseness of judgment, became wicked, rebellious, and obdurate in heart and will, and impure in all his affections."

And in the same chapter, Article 3: "Therefore all men are conceived in sin, and by nature children of wrath, incapable of saving good, prone to evil, dead in sin, and in bondage thereto, and without the regenerating grace of the Holy Spirit, they are neither able nor willing to return to God, to reform the depravity of their nature, nor to dispose themselves to reformation."

26. But does not this last article speak only of the incapa-bility of the natural man to do saving good, thus leaving room at least for the doctrine that he is able to do good in respect to things natural and civil?

Indeed not. Saving good is mentioned with special emphasis because the Canons were composed to gainsay

the error of the Arminians according to which the natural
man is able to improve upon himself and to attain to
saving good by the right use of his natural light. Nevertheless, this is by no means all the Canons here teach. For
they also assert that the sinner is dead in sin, in bondage
thereto, that he cannot will to reform himself, nor to
dispose himself to reformation.

27. What, then, does Article 3 of the Canons III/IV teach?

That there is one and only one way in which fallen
man can be delivered from corruption, and in which he
may be enabled to do good: the way of regeneration by
the Spirit of God. The third point, however, expressly
teaches that there is another way, another influence of
God upon the natural man, that does not regenerate the
heart, but empowers the corrupt tree to bring forth good
fruit in the sphere of things natural and civil.

28. What is the conclusion with respect to the proof synod claimed to find in the Reformed confessions to support its declaration of doctrine in the third point?

That it has utterly failed. Not only are the fragmen-
tary quotations it made utterly wanting in proof, but the
confessions in every one of the three forms of unity
contradict most emphatically the contention that the natural man is able to do good works in the sphere of things
natural and civil, and that through an influence of God
which is not regenerative.

Synod's Proof for the Third Point From Scripture

1. *To what Scripture passages did synod refer in support of the third point?*

To the following:

II Kings 10:29, 30: "Howbeit from the sins of Jeroboam the son of Nebat, who made Israel to sin, Jehu departed not from after them, to wit, the golden calves that were in Bethel, and that were in Dan. And the LORD said unto Jehu, Because thou hast done well in executing that which is right in mine eyes, and hast done unto the house of Ahab according to all that was in mine heart, thy children of the fourth generation shall sit on the throne of Israel."

II Kings 12:2: "And Jehoash did that which was right in the sight of the LORD all his days wherein Jehoiada the priest instructed him."

II Kings 14:3: "And he (Amaziah) did that which was right in the sight of the LORD, yet not like David his father; he did according to all things as Joash his father did." Cf. II Chronicles 25:2: "And he did that which was right in the sight of the LORD, but not with a perfect heart."

Luke 6:33: "And if ye do good to them which do good to you, what thank have ye? for sinners also do even the same."

Romans 2:14: "For when the Gentiles, which have not the law, do by nature the things contained in the law, these, having not the law, are a law unto themselves." Here synod refers us to verse 13: "For not the hearers of

149

the law are just before God, but the doers of the law shall be justified." Also to Romans 10:5: "For Moses describeth the righteousness which is of the law, That the man which doeth those things shall live by them." And to Galatians 3:12: "And the law is not of faith: but, the man that doeth them shall live in them."

2. Does the example of Jehu prove that the natural man, through an influence of the Holy Spirit upon him, receives grace through which he is able to do good?

On the contrary, there is no mention in the text of an operation of the Holy Spirit upon Jehu at all. Nor was any amelioration or restraint of Jehu's wickedness necessary to the performance of his deed.

3. But does not the Lord approve of him as having done well?

Certainly: but this does not concern the point at issue at all. The wicked can do many things well, because of natural talent and ability, while at the same time and with respect to the same things they sin. This is so self-evident that the very simple can readily understand it. A man may be an able business man, so that he handles all his affairs well, and yet he may make all his business subservient to sin. He does well, yet he sins. An able engineer may invent an almost perfect mechanism, and in doing so he certainly does well, yet he may employ all his talents to enhance his own glory or for some other sinful purpose, so that he also sins while he does well. It is even possible that a man may lead a clean moral life to a certain extent, and keep himself from gross outward sins, merely because he knows that a life of corruption leads him to premature destruction. For all of this no ameliorating influence of the Holy Spirit is necessary. A person may perform well a certain piece of work, and yet sin.

This explains exactly the story of Jehu. It is evident that he was a wicked man. For the honor and service of Jehovah he cared not, for he followed after the sins of Jeroboam, the son of Nebat, who made Israel to sin. This is emphasized in the text. Both before and after the statement that he did well it is said that he departed not from the sins of Jeroboam. From this it ought to be evident that he was not actuated by the love of Jehovah in whatever he did well. In the second place, it is also evident that Jehu was an able man, quick to see a situation and to act accordingly, undaunted in battle, thorough in all his work. And the narrative shows that he was ambitious. In the third place, it is more than evident that, in the command of the Lord to extinguish the house of Ahab, Jehu perceived a means to his own advancement and aggrandizement, a way to ascend the throne of Israel.

From this ambition as a motive, one can explain all that Jehu did. What he did he certainly did well. He completely extinguished the house of Ahab. And yet, while he did it, he sinned. This is first of all evident from the repeated statement that he did not depart from the sins of Jeroboam, which proved beyond any doubt that the love of God was not his motive. This is proven, in the second place, from Hosea 1:4: "And the LORD said unto him, Call his name Jezreel, for yet a little while, and I will avenge the blood of Jezreel upon the house of Jehu, and will cause to cease the kingdom of the house of Israel." For the very thing, then, which Jehu did so well, but did wickedly, he was punished as a matter of blood-guiltiness. He received a reward, indeed. And the reward was entirely in accord with the work he had done so well. In four generations he would sit on the throne of Israel. But it was the reward of the wicked, leading him more quickly to destruction. It will then be evident that Jehu's example does not prove the point that the wicked can do good through an influence of God on them.

4. But do not the examples of Jehoash and Amaziah prove such a gracious influence of God upon the natural man?

Indeed not. The right these kings did in the sight of the Lord refers to their reign as kings, particularly to certain reforms they brought about. In the case of Jehoash, however, it is evident that he did right, not from the love of Jehovah, nor from the influence of a certain common grace, but under the influence of Jehoiada the priest. As long as the priest instructed him, he did what was right in the sight of the Lord. And, although we are not informed what motivated Amaziah in the first part of his reign to do what was right in the sight of the Lord (though not with a perfect heart), the examples of Jehu and of Jehoash ought to be sufficient to guard us against the conception that it was due to an influence of the Holy Spirit, improving a natural man without regenerating him.

5. But does not the text from Luke 6:33 plainly state that sinners do good?

On the contrary, it states very plainly that they do no good. That synod could quote passages such as this only proves how desperately hard pressed they were for even a semblance of evidence for the truth of the third point. It appears that, in quoting this text, the learned committee that presented its report on this matter to synod were led astray by the mere sound of the word *good,* and without even seriously reading the text they concluded that here they had indeed found an indubitable proof for the theory that the wicked can do good.

What does the text teach? That sinners can do good? That there is an influence of the Holy Spirit upon them by which they are somewhat improved? To be sure, there is not the slightest reference to these gross errors in the text. The Lord does not declare that sinners do good. He does not even state that they do good to man. Still more, He does not assert that they do good one to another. What He does state is that they do good to them that will reward them with good, that they love those that will love them.

And what is this? Is it good? No, it is mere selfishness of the sinful man. He has no reward. And the Lord uses their examples to warn His disciples not to do good in like manner! I suppose that the more earnest-minded of the synodical delegates, looking back upon 1924, are ashamed of themselves that they could be so led astray by the mere sound of words!

6. But does not Romans 2:14 teach that the Gentiles keep the law?

Considering the additional references to which synod calls our attention, one must, indeed, draw the conclusion that it was synod's intention to teach that the heathen keep the law of God. For it refers to Romans 2:13; 10:5; Galatians 3:12. This is, indeed, a serious heresy; for it denies, as far as the heathen are concerned, the incapability of performing the law of God and the need of redemption. For, according to Romans 2:13, the doers of the law shall be justified, and he that is justified is saved. According to Romans 10:5 and Galatians 3:12, he that doeth these things shall live by them.

If, then, as synod evidently desired to show, the Gentiles keep the law of God and do the things contained in them, they shall be justified and live by the things of the law.

However, this is not the teaching of the Scriptures. Even the general and clear teaching of the Bible ought to have been sufficient to restrain synod from such an interpretation of Romans 2:14. Nor is this at all the true meaning of this passage. When we read that the Gentiles do by nature the things contained in the law, the meaning is not that they keep the law of God, but that they do, without the possession of a revealed law, what the law did for Israel. What does the law do? Distinguish for various departments of life between what is good and evil. This the heathen did for themselves, though they possessed no external, divinely revealed code of precepts.

The original does not read: "the things contained in the law." The heathen, having "the work of the law" written in their hearts (which is quite different from having the law written in their hearts), outlined for themselves laws in which they plainly revealed that they could distinguish between good and evil even without a revealed code.

This does by no means signify that they also kept the law as they knew it, that they did the good, and that, therefore, they were justified. On the contrary, knowing the law, they transgressed, and were left without excuse in the day of the revelation of the righteous judgment of God. Anyone will be able to see and will be compelled to acknowledge that this is the true interpretation of the text and that, in this way, we do not fall into the gross errors of Pelagianism.

7.   Can it, then, be honestly said that synod succeeded in proving its contention of the third point?

On the contrary, though it diligently searched the Scriptures in order to find such proof, it utterly failed.

8.   What can be said as to the positive testimony of the Scriptures regarding the actual iniquity of the natural man?

It is so abundant, and it so flagrantly conflicts with the declaration of the third point, that one can only be amazed at the boldness of synod to maintain its error in the face of it.

9.   Can you quote some of this testimony?

Psalm 14:1-3: "The fool hath said in his heart, There is

no God. They are corrupt, they have done abominable works, there is none that doeth good. The LORD looked down from heaven upon the children of men, to see if there were any that did understand, and seek God. They are all gone aside, they are altogether become filthy: there is none that doeth good, no, not one."

Notice that the language here allows of no exception. All, without the exception of so much as one, have gone out of the way and become filthy. And notice, too, that this does not merely refer to their nature, but also to their actual life and walk in the world. They sin and do nothing but that which is abominable in the sight of the Lord.

10. But does not the above passage of Scripture, and do not similar texts, refer perhaps to special conditions, or to a special class of sinners, without implicating all men?

This view is sometimes broached, but it is plainly contradicted by the Scriptures themselves. Notice that it is exactly this and other passages which the apostle Paul quotes in Romans 3:9-18, and that with application to all men without distinction: "What then? Are we better than they? No, in no wise: for we have before proved both Jews and Gentiles, that they are all under sin; as it is written, There is none righteous, no, not one: There is none that understandeth, there is none that seeketh after God. They are all gone out of the way, they are together become unprofitable; there is none that doeth good, no, not one. Their throat is an open sepulchre; with their tongues they have used deceit; the poison of asps is under their lips: Whose mouth is full of cursing and bitterness: Their feet are swift to shed blood: Destruction and misery are in their ways: And the way of peace have they not known: There is no fear of God before their eyes."

11. Have you any proof to contradict the error of synod expressed in the third point?

In Romans 1:28-32 the apostle is picturing the moral condition of the Roman world at the pinnacle of its civilization. If anywhere in the ancient world there were visible fruits of the highly lauded influence of common grace, they are to be sought in the world of Graeco-Roman culture. And what does the apostle write of that world? Listen: "And even as they did not like to retain God in their knowledge, God gave them over to a reprobate mind, to do those things which are not convenient; being filled with all unrighteousness, fornication, wickedness, covetousness, maliciousness; full of envy, murder, debate, deceit, malignity; whisperers, backbiters, haters of God, despiteful, proud, boasters, inventors of evil things, disobedient to parents, without understanding, covenant-breakers, without natural affection, implacable, unmerciful: Who knowing the judgment of God, that they which commit such things are worthy of death, not only do the same, but have pleasure in them that do them."

12. Can you quote still more?

Yes, the Lord teaches in Matthew 7:16-20: "Ye shall know them by their fruits. Do men gather grapes of thorns, or figs of thistles? Even so every good tree bringeth forth good fruit; but a corrupt tree bringeth forth evil fruit. A good tree cannot bring forth evil fruit, neither can a corrupt tree bring forth good fruit. Every tree that bringeth not forth good fruit is hewn down, and cast into the fire. Wherefore by their fruits ye shall know them."

These words of the Savior are clearly contradicted by the third declaration of the synod of 1924. For it teaches plainly that grapes may be gathered from thorns and figs from thistles and good works from wicked men. It surely maintains that a corrupt tree can, indeed, bring forth good fruit, and this by a gracious influence of the Holy Spirit upon the corrupt tree. Its teaching makes it forevermore impossible to know men by their fruits. Is this not also clearly taught by many defenders of the theory of common grace? Do they not maintain that the lives of the wicked in this world often put to shame the lives of the children of God? How, then, would it be possible to distinguish a tree by its fruit, if the Holy Spirit by a work of grace gives to the corrupt tree the appearance of the good?

13. Is not the teaching of the third point also plainly contradicted by the testimony of the truth in the believing consciousness of the Christian?

Indeed, it is. For, the Christian, who by the grace of God has come to the true knowledge of himself, must confess that his best works are defiled with sin, that his righteousnesses are nothing but a filthy garment, that outside of Christ he lies in the midst of death. And, finding this testimony concerning himself in his own heart, it is impossible for him to believe that the natural man may still do much good in the sight of God.

14. What, then, is the truth concerning the natural man?

This, that he is by nature incapable of doing any good and inclined to all evil, that he is darkened in his understanding, hardened of heart, perverse of will, a corrupt tree, and that as such he always brings forth corrupt fruit, without exception. We deny that there is an ameliorating influence of the Holy Spirit upon him, through which he is able to do the good. We deny that in actual fact he ever does what is good.

This does not mean that we deny that the natural man often tries to adapt his life and walk in the world according to the law of God as he knows it. This he certainly does, because he perceives that he cannot escape that law, and that an outward adaptation of himself to that law is not only good for him, but also necessary.

Man in the state of righteousness was king-servant of

God over and in the midst of all the earthly creation. His position was such that all creatures must serve him, that he might serve his God. Through the fall, however, he radically changed in his relation to God. The servant of God became a rebel against Him; the friend of God changed into His enemy. His knowledge became darkness, his righteousness iniquity, his holiness corruption and rebellion against God. Yet, he still stood in the midst of creation. This relation was, indeed, marred; but it was not broken. The ungodly is still king in relation to all earthly creatures. As such he attempts to maintain himself in and through the earthly *kosmos,* over against God. He still insists that the creature shall serve him; but with that creature he serves sin, the devil.

Also that earthly creation, however, his own life included, is bound by the law of God. It exists and develops according to God's ordinances. And the natural man, perceiving this relation, knowing that he is bound by the law of God on all sides, understanding, too, that the law of God is his preservation, has a certain regard for external virtue and discipline. Formally and externally, though inwardly he is an enemy of God, he attempts to conform his life and existence to the law of God. In this attempt he sometimes is successful in a measure. More often he fails, and ultimately will utterly fail. In as far as he succeeds, he lives in temperance, world-peace, and social security. But in the measure that he fails, he reveals that he is a glutton and adulterer, a thief and murderer, a liar and covenant-breaker; he is swift to shed blood; he leaves destruction in his ways; he causes war and revolution. But whether he succeeds or fails in this attempt, always he is the enemy of God and the friend of the devil. The good he never performs. Only by the wonder of God's grace, through the regenerative and sanctifying power of the Holy Spirit in Christ Jesus, our Lord, is he changed into a good tree that bringeth forth good fruit.

It is for this good confession that the Christian Reformed Church in 1924 cast out their Protestant Reformed brethren.

Theirs only is the blame for the breach that was caused!

Section III

A Catechism
on the
Doctrinal Issues
of 1953

Herman Hanko

Historical Background

1. What were the historical roots of the controversy that led to a split in the Protestant Reformed Churches in 1953?

The doctrinal controversy in the Reformed Churches of the Netherlands which took place in the first part of the 20th century.

2. What was the historical background of this controversy in the Netherlands?

In 1834 Hendrik DeCock and other ministers led a separation from the state church to establish a new denomination. This separation is generally known as *De Afscheiding,* which means "The Separation." In 1886 Dr. Abraham Kuyper led another separation from the state church, which was called *De Doleantie,* or, "The Grievance." In 1892, although significant doctrinal differences were present between these two groups, they merged into a new denomination called "The Reformed Churches in the Netherlands."

3. What were some of the doctrinal differences between these two groups?

The "Separated Churches" held to mediate regeneration, infra-lapsarianism, and temporal justification, and many held also to a general and conditional promise of the covenant. The "Aggrieved Churches" held to immediate regeneration, supra-lapsarianism, eternal justification, and presupposed regeneration.

4. What part of these doctrinal differences were especially the historical roots of the controversy in the Protestant Reformed Churches in 1953?

The doctrine of the promise of God's covenant and its relation to the grounds for infant baptism. Dr. Abraham Kuyper held to the position that infants born within the covenant must be baptized on the ground of presupposed regeneration; i.e., believing parents presuppose that their children are regenerated. The view more generally held among the churches of the Separation was that children of believing parents must be baptized on the ground that the promise of salvation was for all the children of believers, but it was conditioned by faith.

5. What was the result of this controversy in the Netherlands?

Dr. Klaas Schilder was deposed from his office as professor in the Kampen Theological School and as emeritus minister of the congregation in Delftshaven, by the Synod of Sneek-Utrecht in 1942 - 1944.

6. What was the outcome of Dr. Schilder's deposition?

A new denomination was formed called "The Reformed Churches of the Netherlands, Maintaining Article 31 of the Church Order." This denomination is more commonly known as the "Liberated Churches."

7. How was this controversy in the Netherlands related to the controversy in the Protestant Reformed Churches?

Dr. Schilder came twice to this country, once in 1939 prior to his deposition, and again in 1947.

8. Did Dr. Schilder have any contact with the Protestant Reformed Churches?

He did. He preached and lectured in various Protestant Reformed congregations throughout the country.

9. Why were the pulpits of the Protestant Reformed Churches opened to Dr. Schilder?

This was done chiefly because the pulpits in the Christian Reformed Church were closed to him.

10. Were there other reasons?

Yes; a kinship had developed between Rev. Herman Hoeksema and Dr. Schilder because both men had been unjustly deposed from office by broader ecclesiastical assemblies, and because there was some agreement with them on the subject of the rejection of common grace.

11. Were Rev. Hoeksema and Dr. Schilder aware of differences in their covenant views?

Yes, they were, but it was hoped that through personal contact and discussion these differences could be overcome and agreement reached on these important doctrines.

12. Were these hopes of agreement realized?

No, they were not. The differences were great and proved to be beyond resolution.

13. What were these differences?

a. The idea of the covenant. The Protestant Reformed Churches maintained that the covenant was a bond of friendship and fellowship between God and His elect people in Christ. Dr. Schilder made the essence of the covenant the promises and demands of the covenant.

b. The promise of the covenant. The Protestant Reformed Churches held to the view that the promise of the covenant is for the elect only. Dr. Schilder maintained that the promise of the covenant is for all that are born in the line of the covenant.

c. The unconditionality of the promise. The Protestant Reformed Churches maintained that the promise of God's covenant is completely unconditional. Dr. Schilder maintained that the promise of the covenant is conditional. That is, Dr. Schilder maintained that, while the promise of the covenant is for all children of believers, this promise is actually fulfilled for those who believe in Christ and thus fulfill the conditions of the covenant.

d. The realization of the covenant. The Protestant Reformed Churches held that there can be no *parties* in the covenant, but that those who are saved are called to obedience. Dr. Schilder maintained that God and man were both parties in the covenant.

14. Did Dr. Schilder's views of the covenant have any influence in the Protestant Reformed Churches?
Yes. Many ministers, officebearers, and members adopted Dr. Schilder's position, and began to teach Dr. Schilder's views in the churches.

15. What added factor led to Dr. Schilder's influence in the Protestant Reformed Churches?
After World War II many immigrants came to Canada and the United States. The immigrants from the Liberated Churches were looking for a church home and wanted to become a part of the Protestant Reformed Churches, if they could maintain their covenant views. Many in the Protestant Reformed Churches were willing to leave these questions open so that Liberated immigrants would be free to join.

16. What aggravated these problems?
In 1949 two Protestant Reformed ministers visited the Netherlands and, in conferences with Liberated ministers

and theologians, insisted that the Protestant Reformed Churches had room for the covenant views of Liberated people.

17. Were Protestant Reformed Churches organized from Liberated immigrants?

Yes, two were organized: one in Chatham, Ontario and another in Hamilton, Ontario.

18. What event brought the differences between the two denominations to a head?

The adoption of *A Brief Declaration of Principles of the Protestant Reformed Churches*, (cf. Appendix, p. 203) provisionally adopted by the synod of 1950 and finally adopted by the synod of 1951.

19. What is the Declaration of Principles?

It is a document adopted by the synod of the Protestant Reformed Churches to be used in mission work, particularly among the Liberated, which sets forth the teachings of the Reformed confessions on the doctrines of common grace, the free offer of the gospel, and the unconditionality and particularity of the promises of the covenant.

20. What other events took place which revealed the differences in covenant views among the members of the Protestant Reformed Churches?

The introduction of a new paper, *Concordia*, which was used for the purpose of defending Liberated theology and which took issue with the distinct covenant views of the Protestant Reformed Churches.

21. What events brought the controversy to the ecclesiastical assemblies?

The preaching of two sermons by Rev. H. DeWolf

in the First Protestant Reformed Church of Grand Rapids, Michigan. Rev. H. DeWolf was co-pastor with Rev. H. Hoeksema and Rev. C. Hanko in the mother church and largest congregation of the Protestant Reformed Churches.

22. Why did these sermons create further divisions?

In the first sermon, preached April 15, 1951 on Luke 19:19-31, Rev. DeWolf made the following statement: "God promises every one of you that if you believe, you will be saved." In the second sermon, preached September 14, 1952 on Matthew 18:3, Rev. DeWolf said: "Our act of conversion is a prerequisite to enter the kingdom."

23. How did these statements bring the issues to a head?

Various protests were lodged against them by members of the congregation. After months of discussion and debate in the consistory over the orthodoxy of these statements, the matter came to Classis East in April of 1953.

24. What did classis decide?

Classis decided that these statements were not Reformed according to Scripture and the Reformed confessions and that Rev. DeWolf must apologize for them or be suspended from his office of minister of the Word.

25. Did Rev. DeWolf apologize as classis required?

Although Rev. DeWolf offered what he called an apology, this apology was not acceptable to the consistory, and Rev. DeWolf was suspended from office in June of 1953.

26. How did this suspension of Rev. DeWolf lead to the split in the churches?

Those in Classis East and in Classis West who supported the views of Rev. DeWolf left the denomination to form a denomination of their own.

27. Did many in the churches follow those who left?

Yes, more than half of the membership of the Protestant Reformed Churches left the denomination.

28. Did these churches which left maintain their separate identity?

No, these churches returned to the Christian Reformed Church in 1961.

29. Have the Protestant Reformed Churches continued their existence?

Yes, they have. The truths of sovereign and particular grace are, by God's grace and mercy, maintained by them to the present.

The Truth
of the Covenant

1.   What was the central truth at issue in the controversy of 1953?

The truth concerning God's everlasting covenant of grace.

2.   What was the view of the covenant held throughout much of the history of the Reformed churches?

That the covenant of grace is a pact or agreement between God and man.

3.   What are the elements of that agreement between God and man?

God and man enter into an agreement which contains mutual promises, conditions, threats, and obligations, all of which are a part of the ratification of the covenant.

4.   What are some of these promises, conditions, and obligations?

On God's part, God promises to bless man with the blessings of salvation and eternal life in heaven on the condition of faith and obedience, assumes the responsibility of sending Christ to die for sin, by whose death salvation is accomplished, and threatens man with eternal punishment should man break God's covenant. Man, on his part, agrees to the terms of the covenant, promises

to accept Christ by faith, walk in obedience before God,
and fulfill the obligations laid upon him.

5. How was this covenant revealed?

It was revealed in Paradise as a covenant of works;
but, because Adam broke that covenant, it is now revealed as a covenant of grace, although the basic structure
of the covenant as an agreement remains.

6. What objections can be raised against this view of the covenant?

The objections are many and serious.

a. That God and man enter together into an agreement
places God and man on the same level, for only equals
enter into agreements. The vast gulf which separates the
triune God from puny man is bridged.

b. It introduces into the idea of the covenant the
Arminian conception that God is dependent upon man
for the realization of His covenant. God will not ratify His
covenant unless man agrees to and fulfills the conditions
of the covenant.

c. It leaves no room for children of believers in the
covenant, for children cannot enter into an agreement.

d. It is a mechanical view of the covenant which
reduces the covenant of grace to a mere formal pact.

7. What is the scriptural teaching concerning the nature of God's covenant of grace?

Scripture teaches that the covenant of grace is a relationship of friendship and fellowship which God establishes between Himself and His people in Christ, in which
He is their God and they are His people.

8. Can you prove that this is the biblical idea of the covenant?

Yes, for the relationship between the saints and God is described in such covenantal terms. Enoch "walked with God" (Gen. 5:22); Noah walked with God (Gen. 6:9); Abraham was called the "friend of God" (Jam. 2:23).

9. Can you give more proof?
Yes, in Psalm 25:14 the covenant is defined in terms of God revealing His secret to them that fear Him.

10. Is still more proof to be found in Scripture?
Yes, when the covenant is described, it is described in terms of a relationship in which God is the God of His people and His people belong to Him (Gen. 17:7, II Cor. 6:16-18). The final perfection of the covenant is defined in terms of God's tabernacle with men, in which He will dwell with His people (Rev. 21:3, 4). That God dwells with His people was foreshadowed by the temple (II Chron. 7:1-3), realized in the incarnation of our Lord Jesus Christ (Matt. 1:23), and accomplished by the Spirit in the hearts of the elect, by whom they are made one with Christ (I Cor. 12:12, 13).

11. Why is this view of Scripture so beautiful?
Scripture speaks throughout of a relationship of friendship between God and His people in Christ, so that salvation, when defined in terms of the covenant, is a warm and living truth in which God's people become the friends of God.

12. Is this truth of the covenant rooted in God Himself?
Yes, it is. God is in His own triune life a covenant God in which the three Persons of the holy Trinity dwell together in friendship and fellowship.

13. How does this relate to the covenant of grace?
God takes His people, through Christ, into His own

triune covenant life so that they even become "partakers of the divine nature" (II Pet. 1:4).

14. What other figure does Scripture use to describe the covenant?

It uses the figure of a family. God is a family God in which the triune God is the Father of Jesus Christ. Through the establishment of the covenant of grace, God establishes His own family of the elect in which He is their Father, Christ is the elder Brother, and all the people of God are sons and daughters dwelling together in fellowship (II Cor. 6:18).

15. Is the establishment of this covenant the work of God and man?

No, it is not. God sovereignly and graciously establishes His covenant by His own work of grace in such a way that His elect people are taken into His covenant by His own sovereign power. This is clearly taught in the establishment of the covenant with Abraham (Gen. 15:9-18), in which passage we are told that Abraham was asleep when God established His covenant with him.

16. Is the continuation of the covenant the work of man?

Scripture teaches us clearly that it is not. When God established His covenant with David, God told David that He would continue His covenant even though David and his seed sinned (Ps. 89:19-37).

17. But does not Psalm 89 speak of the establishment of the covenant with Christ?

Indeed it does. But though Christ is the seed of David with whom the covenant is first of all established, all those who believe are in Christ, the seed of Abraham and heirs of the covenant (Gal. 3:16, 29).

18. Does man himself then do anything either to ratify the covenant or to guarantee that it is continued?

He does not. God sovereignly establishes the covenant by His grace and preserves His elect in that covenant through His power.

19. But does not the believer have obligations in the covenant?

Yes, he does, as our baptism form clearly indicates when it speaks of our "part" in the covenant.

20. How is this to be explained?

The baptism form does not speak of "parties" in the covenant, as if the covenant were an agreement between God and man, but it speaks of "parts" in the covenant. Our "part" of the covenant is our obligation to walk in obedience to God, by which we express our gratitude to God for His salvation. But even this gratitude to God we show by the grace which God gives us as those who are taken into His covenant.

21. Are children of believers also included in the covenant?

This is the clear teaching of our confessions and baptism form. Our Heidelberg Catechism states that "they, as well as the adult, are included in the covenant and church of God" (A. 74). Our baptism form says that we may not exclude our children from baptism because, "as they are without their knowledge, partakers of the condemnation in Adam, so are they again received unto grace in Christ."

22. Does this mean that children are also regenerated and given faith?

As a general rule the children of believers are also saved in infancy. Our baptism form teaches this when it

asks believing parents whether they acknowledge that
their children "are sanctified in Christ" and are "members
of Christ's church."

23. Is this also proved by Scripture?

Jeremiah was sanctified before he was born (Jer. 1:5);
John the Baptist acknowledged the presence of the mother
of the Lord by leaping in his mother's womb (Luke 1:41);
the law is addressed to children who are saved (Ex. 20:1,
12, Deut. 5:6, 16); Paul includes injunctions to children
who are saints (Eph. 1:1 & 6:1-3, Col. 1:2 & 3:20); Jesus
received little children and blessed them (Mark 10:13-16);
and Peter speaks of the promise of God for children who
are called (Acts 2:39).

24. Does all this mean that all the children of believers are saved?

No, it does not, for Esau was born of believing parents
and yet was reprobate; and Paul specifically says that
"they are not all Israel, which are of Israel" (Rom. 9:6).
Only the elect children of believers are saved.

25. Does not God save outside of covenant generations?

Yes, through the work of missions God gathers new
generations into the covenant and saves parents and their
children by missionary work (Acts 16:31, 34; I Cor. 1:16).

26. How does the truth that God saves believers and their seed relate to the sacrament of baptism?

Children of believers are to be baptized because they
as well as adults are included in the covenant of God.

27. What did Abraham Kuyper teach concerning the ground for the baptism of infants?

He taught that all the children of believers must be
baptized because we are to "presuppose" that all are truly

saved. This was called the doctrine of "presupposed regeneration."

28. Do the Protestant Reformed Churches believe in presupposed regeneration?

No, they do not, although it is commonly alleged that they do.

29. What is wrong about the doctrine of presupposed regeneration?

It presupposes that something is true which Scripture says is not true. It presupposes that all children of believers are saved, when Scripture tells us that not all that are of Israel are truly Israel.

30. Can you mention a practical consequence of this erroneous doctrine?

If parents presuppose that all their children are saved, they will not warn their children who walk in sin, and the church will not discipline wayward members.

31. Why are parents obligated to instruct all their children in the fear of the Lord when they know that some may not be true children of God?

Parents are unable to know who of their children are true believers and who are not, and so must give covenant instruction to them all.

32. Is it also the will of God that all the children receive such instruction?

Yes, this is clear from Scripture. Scripture enjoins us to teach all our children the ways of God's covenant (Gen. 18:17-19; Prov. 22:6; and many other passages in Scripture).

33. Does God have His purpose also in this?

Yes, for, just as in the preaching of the gospel elect and reprobate must come under the preaching and receive its outward benefits, so also must all the children of the covenant receive covenant instruction.

34. Can you explain this further?

God wills that the "rain" of the preaching and baptism come upon all, that the carnal seed may manifest itself as wicked (Is. 55:10, 11; Heb. 6:7, 8). This is also taught in John 15:1-7, where branches which are in the vine must be cut out.

35. Does God teach this same truth in His creation?

Yes; the farmer fertilizes and waters his entire field, even though he knows that the result will be that thorns and weeds will grow as well as his wheat and corn. But the wheat is harvested and the thorns are burned. So also a corn stalk grows to produce only a small amount of corn, while much of the plant is burned or plowed back into the ground.

36. What do the Liberated teach concerning the ground for infant baptism?

They teach that all children are objectively included in the covenant, and all objectively receive the blessings of the covenant.

37. Are not all children saved then?

No, when children come to years of discretion they must accept the conditions of the covenant. If they do not, they are covenant-breakers.

38. Can you illustrate this?

All children when baptized receive a "check" from God which reads: "Pay to the order of [the child baptized] the sum of salvation." A child can, when he grows up, do one of three things with that check:

a. He can hang it in a frame on the wall, in which case it will do him no good (he is a hypocrite in the church).

b. He can rip it up and throw it away, in which case he is a covenant breaker.

c. He can cash it in the bank of heaven, in which case the blessings of the covenant will actually become his.

39. What is the error of this position?

It proceeds from the assumption that the covenant is conditional; for only when the conditions of the covenant are met will a child actually be saved.

40. What else can be said about this view?

It considers children of believing parents to be unbelievers until such a time as they fulfill the conditions of the covenant, and they must be treated as unbelievers, for children are unable to fulfill any conditions.

41. Is there a still more serious objection?

Yes, it introduces into the covenant the age-old error of Arminianism, because the actual realization of the covenant is dependent on man. He must fulfill the conditions of the covenant before the covenant will actually be his.

42. But can it not be argued that God fulfills the condition by His grace?

No, for it is absurd to say that God promises salvation on the condition that He will fulfill it.

43. Is a conditional promise a serious error?

Yes, it is, for it denies the truth of the absolute sovereignty of God in the work of salvation.

The Issues of the Controversy

1. Were the doctrines of the nature of God's covenant and the ground for the baptism of infants also issues in 1953?

Yes, they were, for those in the Protestant Reformed Churches who departed from the truth held basically the views of the Liberated Churches, who taught that the covenant is an agreement between God and man and who believe that all the children of believers are included in the covenant.

2. What was the first statement which Rev. DeWolf made which led to his deposition?

"God promises to every one of you that, if you believe, you will be saved."

3. But did not this statement have to do with the preaching of the gospel and not with the doctrine of the covenant?

It did; but Rev. DeWolf applied the idea of a general and conditional promise in the covenant also to the preaching of the gospel.

4. Show how this is true.

The Liberated view of the covenant teaches that in baptism God promises every baptized child that if he will believe, he will be saved. DeWolf applied the same principle to the preaching generally: In the preaching

God promises every one who hears the preaching that, if he believes, he will be saved.

5. Are the sacrament of baptism and the preaching of the gospel related?
Yes, they are. The sacrament of baptism is added to the preaching as a sign and a seal of the truths of the gospel.

6. Why is this statement contrary to the Scriptures and the Reformed confessions?
It teaches that the promise of God is general and conditional.

7. What do you mean that the promise of God is general?
That the promise of salvation in Christ is given to every one who is baptized or hears the preaching.

8. Was this indeed the teaching of Rev. DeWolf?
Yes, it was. He stated emphatically that the promise is "to every one of you," i.e., to every one, elect and reprobate, who hears the preaching.

9. Would this not mean that every one who hears the preaching is saved?
No, it does not; for a condition is added: "If you believe, you will be saved."

10. How do a general promise and a conditional promise belong together?
Those who teach a general promise recognize that not all who hear the gospel (or who are baptized) are actually saved. To explain why all are not actually saved, a condition is added to limit the scope of salvation to those who believe.

11. How is this similar to the Liberated doctrine of a general and conditional promise in baptism?

The Liberated teach that the promise in baptism is given to all the children baptized, but it is realized only on condition of faith. That is, the promise is actually given to those children who, when they grow up, fulfill the condition of faith.

12. Why is this view Arminian in its teaching?

It makes faith the work of man and salvation dependent upon man's believing.

13. Explain this more fully.

All who hear the preaching and are baptized receive God's promise so that it is actually their own, although this is true only objectively. To receive this promise subjectively, they must fulfill the condition of faith.

14. But cannot it be said that the fulfillment of this condition is God's work?

No, it cannot. Faith is described in Scripture as *a part of salvation* (Eph. 2:8). If it is a part of salvation, it cannot be *a condition to* salvation.

15. Illustrate this.

If I promise twenty crippled people in the room that I will give them $1000.00 if they walk a mile, the condition to receiving the gift is their ability to walk the mile I require. This condition is not a part of the gift, but a condition to receiving it. Faith cannot be a condition to salvation and a part of salvation at the same time.

16. But could not this statement be interpreted to mean that God always saved His people in the way of faith?

No. This would make the statement of Rev. DeWolf meaningless at best and teaching a universal salvation at worst. The statement would then read: "God promises to every one of you that He will save you in the way of faith."

17. But do not the Scriptures say: "Believe on the Lord Jesus Christ and thou shalt be saved?"

Yes, they do, but this is a command of God which comes to all and which requires of all that they believe in Christ. It does not teach that God's promise is to every one who hears the gospel upon condition of faith.

18. What is the promise of God from a formal point of view?

It is an oath which God swears by Himself because He can swear by none higher: "For when God made promise to Abraham, because he could swear by no greater, he sware by himself" (Heb. 6:13).

19. What is the promise of God from the point of view of its contents?

It is the promise of salvation in Christ: "Surely blessing I will bless thee, and multiplying I will multiply thee" (Heb. 6:14).

20. Can this promise of God be altered in any way?

Hebrews 6:16-18 teaches that it cannot: "For men verily swear by the greater: and an oath for confirmation is to them an end of all strife. Wherein God, willing more abundantly to shew unto the heirs of promise the immutability of his counsel, confirmed it by an oath: that by two immutable things, in which it was impossible for God to lie, we might have a strong consolation, who have fled for refuge to lay hold upon the hope set before us."

21. Is this promise of salvation in Christ for everyone?

No, it is not. Acts 2:39 teaches that it is only for those whom God calls: "For the promise is unto you, and to your children, and to all that are afar off, even as many as the Lord our God shall call."

22. Is this promise conditioned on the faith of man?

No, for faith also is the gift of God: "For by grace are ye saved through faith; and that not of yourselves: it is the gift of God" (Eph. 2:8).

23. How did DeWolf make it clear that he was Arminian in his view of salvation?

He did this by the second statement for which he was condemned: "Our act of conversion is a prerequisite to enter the kingdom."

24. Why was this clearly Arminian?

It taught that conversion is our act and not God's gift. Further, it taught that our act was required for entrance into the kingdom of Christ.

25. What is the meaning of "prerequisite"?

The term "prerequisite" is not a biblical term. Webster's Collegiate Dictionary defines "prerequisite" as: "Required before; necessary as a preliminary to a proposed effect or end; essential as a condition precedent."

26. What is the kingdom of heaven?

It is the kingdom which God establishes through the blood of Christ shed on Calvary, which has as its central character the perfect righteousness of Christ, and which shall be perfectly realized when Christ comes again. It is heavenly in character and includes as its blessings all the gifts of salvation.

27. How does one enter that kingdom?

One enters that kingdom through the work of God: "[God] hath delivered us from the power of darkness, and hath translated us into the kingdom of his dear Son" (Col. 1:13).

28. What is conversion?

Our Heidelberg Catechism defines conversion as "the mortification of the old, and the quickening of the new man" (L.D. XXXIII A. 88).

29. What is meant by the mortification of the old, and the quickening of the new man?

The Heidelberg Catechism explains these terms to mean: "a sincere sorrow of heart, that we have provoked God by our sins; and more and more to hate and flee from them"; and, "a sincere joy of heart in God, through Christ, and with love and delight to live according to the will of God in all good works" (L.D. XXXIII A. 89, 90).

30. Is this conversion the work of God?

The Canons teach that it is: "But when God accomplishes his good pleasure in the elect, or works in them true conversion ..." (Canons III/IV, 11). The Canons expressly condemn the Arminian position that conversion is the work of man in III/IV, B, 6, 7.

31. Where does Scripture teach that conversion is the only way to enter the kingdom of heaven?

In Matthew 18:3, the text on which DeWolf was preaching when he made his heretical statement: "Verily I say unto you, Except ye be converted, and become as little children, ye shall not enter into the kingdom of heaven."

32. But some commentators claim that the words "Except ye be converted" can also be translated "Except ye convert yourselves."

It is indeed possible to translate the text in this way. Surely, if conversion is a sorrow for sin and a delight to live according to the will of God, conversion is also our act.

33. But is it not then possible to give a good interpretation to DeWolf's statement: "Our act of conversion is a prerequisite to enter the kingdom"?

No, this cannot be. In the first place, God works in us our activity of conversion: "For it is God which worketh in you both to will and to do of his good pleasure" (Phil. 2:13). In the second place, this activity which God works in us is not a prerequisite to enter the kingdom of heaven. We are in the kingdom already when we are given the blessing of conversion. Conversion is one of the blessings of the kingdom.

34. What then does Matthew 18:3 mean when it says: "Except ye be converted, and become as little children, ye shall not enter into the kingdom of heaven?"

These words of Jesus refer to the *conscious enjoyment* in this life of the blessings of the kingdom. Only in the way of conversion do we consciously experience the blessedness of being in the kingdom.

35. Was Classis East correct when it spoke of this statement as heretical?

Indeed it was. The statement is openly Arminian, because it teaches that we must convert ourselves before we can enter into the kingdom, thus making conversion our work and not the work of God.

The Question of Conditions

1. *What was the central issue in the entire controversy?*
The central issue was the question whether salvation is conditional or unconditional.

2. *How was this evident?*
The Liberated view of the covenant was a conditional one in which the general promise given in baptism was conditioned on faith. Rev. DeWolf made faith a condition for receiving the promise in his first statement, and made conversion a condition for entrance into the kingdom of heaven in his second statement.

3. *What is meant by the term "condition"?*
The term is not found in Scripture in connection with the work of salvation. Webster's Collegiate Dictionary defines condition as: "1. Something established or agreed upon as a requisite to the doing or taking effect of something else; a stipulation or provision; hence, an agreement determining one or more such prerequisite. 2. That which exists as an occasion of something else; a prerequisite."

4. *What is meant when the term "condition" is applied to the work of salvation?*
When faith is made a condition, the meaning is that salvation will not be granted to anyone unless he fulfills the condition of faith. Man must first believe for salvation to be given to him.

5. But did not earlier theologians use the word "condition" to mean "necessary means"?

Yes, but when the term "condition" is applied to the work of salvation in connection with a general promise, it can no longer refer to "means."

6. What was one of the main arguments raised in support of a conditional salvation?

The use of conditional sentences in Scripture, of which there are many. We may quote two as examples. In Deuteronomy 7:12, 13 we read: "Wherefore it shall come to pass, if ye hearken to these judgments, and keep, and do them, that the LORD thy God shall keep unto thee the covenant and the mercy which he sware unto thy fathers: and he will love thee, and bless thee, and multiply thee: he will also bless the fruit of thy womb, and the fruit of thy land, thy corn, and thy wine, and thine oil, the increase of thy kine, and the flocks of thy sheep, in the land which he sware unto thy fathers to give thee." In Romans 10:9 we read: "That if thou shalt confess with thy mouth the Lord Jesus, and shalt believe in thine heart that God hath raised him from the dead, thou shalt be saved."

7. What other argument from Scripture was used to support a conditional salvation?

Many passages in Scripture can be quoted to prove that the command of the gospel is that one must believe in order to be saved. Paul commanded the Philippian jailor: "Believe on the Lord Jesus Christ, and thou shalt be saved, and thy house" (Acts 16:31).

8. Are there still more such passages?

Yes, in John 3:16 Jesus says: "For God so loved the world, that he gave his only begotten Son, that whosoever believeth in him should not perish, but have everlasting life." The argument is that faith is a condition to everlasting life.

9. What other arguments were raised to support the idea of a conditional salvation?

It was argued that to deny that faith is a condition to salvation is to deny that man has any responsibility to believe. Without such responsibility, man becomes a stock and a block, and salvation is mechanical and apart from man's work altogether.

10. Do such conditional sentences as are found in Deuteronomy 7:12, 13 teach a conditional salvation?

It is important to understand that these passages in the Old Testament were written while Israel was under the law. It certainly was a requirement of the law that the one who kept the law would live: "The man that doeth them shall live in them" (Gal. 3:12). But Israel could not keep the law, and so received the curses of the law instead of its blessings. These curses culminated in the captivity of the nation.

11. Did God intend that Israel should be saved through observance of the law?

No, Paul himself says: "For as many as are of the works of the law are under the curse: for it is written, Cursed is every one that continueth not in all things which are written in the book of the law to do them. But that no man is justified by the law in the sight of God, it is evident: for, The just shall live by faith. And the law is not of faith: but, The man that doeth them shall live in them. Christ hath redeemed us from the curse of the law, being made a curse for us: for it is written, Cursed is every one that hangeth on a tree" (Gal. 3:10-13).

12. Did the law then serve no good purpose?

The law was a schoolmaster to bring God's people to Christ, so that they were justified by faith (Gal. 3:24).

13. But what about the New Testament, and such passages as Romans 10:9, 10?

Not all passages in the New Testament which make use of a conditional sentence refer to a possible condition. The Greek New Testament uses two different words for "if." One of them simply means to assert that the "if-clause" is a reality. This is, e.g., the meaning of Colossians 3:1: "If ye then be risen with Christ, seek those things which are above, where Christ sitteth on the right hand of God." The meaning here is: "Because you are risen with Christ, seek those things which are above."

14. Is this also the meaning of the passage in Romans 10:9, 10?

No, a different word is used here for "if." The word here means that those who do confess with their mouth and believe in their hearts the Lord Jesus will be saved; those who do not believe this will perish.

15. Can Romans 10:9, 10 then be interpreted as referring to faith as a condition to salvation?

No, it cannot. The text means to identify those who. are saved. They are believers who confess with their mouth the Lord Jesus. Only believers are saved.

16. But does not this verse teach that faith is necessary to salvation?

This verse clearly teaches that faith is the means which God uses to save His people.

17. Where is this taught in Scripture?

It is taught in Ephesians 2:8: "For by grace are ye

saved *through faith;* and that not of yourselves: it is the gift of God."

18. Why is faith the means of salvation?

Faith is the God-given gift which unites us to Christ and by which the life of Christ comes to us, so that all the blessings of salvation are given us by Christ. Our Heidelberg Catechism teaches this in L.D. 7, Q. & A. 20: "Are all men then, as they perished in Adam, saved by Christ? No; only those who are ingrafted into him, and receive all his benefits, by a true faith."

19. Is faith then the work of man?

No, it is not. It is God's gift, as Ephesians 2:8 teaches.

20. Why then cannot faith be a condition to salvation?

Faith is one of the blessings of salvation, included in salvation, and a part of salvation.

21. Why then does Scripture speak of faith as the way to salvation?

Scripture does this because it is God's purpose to give us the blessings of salvation in such a way that we consciously experience them. God works that faith in our hearts by which we come to Christ, embrace Him as our only Savior, and find in Him all our salvation. In this way we are given the conscious experience of salvation.

22. Does Acts 16:30 teach that faith is a condition?

No, it does not. It is the command to believe in Christ which comes to all who hear the gospel. When that command of the gospel comes through the preaching, God so works by His Spirit in the hearts of His people that they believe in Christ, receive Him as their Savior, and receive, by faith in Christ, the blessings of salvation.

23. Does John 3:16 teach a conditional salvation?

No. John 3:16 teaches that only believers are saved. And believers are the elect in whom God works faith.

24. But does not the passage teach that God loves all men?

No, it cannot teach this; for, if God loved all men, all men would be saved. The "world" of which Jesus speaks is the world of elect believers.

25. Does not this doctrine rob man of any responsibility?

The wicked are surely accountable before God for their unbelief and will perish in hell. The elect believers are responsible before God for believing and walking in love and obedience. But they are enabled to do this by God's grace.

26. Do believers have the conscious assurance of their salvation when they walk in sin?

This cannot be, for sin always separates us from God and the conscious enjoyment of His salvation. But when God's people walk in sin, God brings them back to Him in the way of repentance and confession of sin, so that they may flee to the cross for forgiveness and find joy in the finished work of Christ.

27. But cannot the idea of faith as a condition to salvation simply mean that faith is the means or way in which God saves?

Although the term has sometimes been used this way, this is not its accepted meaning, and it ought not therefore be used by us in this sense.

28. Do either Scripture or our Reformed confessions use the term condition?

Nowhere in Scripture is the term used at all, much less

as a condition for salvation. Nor do our confessions use the term, except in the Canons, where the term is used to describe the Arminian position. It is used in I, B, 2-5 to describe the heresy of conditional election as taught by the Arminians. It is used in II, B, 3 to describe the heresy of conditional salvation as taught by the Arminians.

29. What then is the character of God's work of salvation?

This salvation is worked by God absolutely unconditionally. God regenerates, gives faith by which we believe, turns us from sin when we fall, brings us to repentance and conversion, preserves us infallibly, and finally takes us to Himself in glory.

The Relation Between 1924 and 1953

1. Was the controversy in the Protestant Reformed Churches in 1953 over conditional salvation related to the controversy in 1924 over common grace?

Yes, it was. The issues were principally the same.

2. What doctrine of common grace was closely related to the doctrines of conditionality?

Especially the teaching of the Christian Reformed Church concerning the free offer of the gospel.

3. What does the free offer of the gospel teach?

That God, in the preaching of the gospel, expresses His desire to save all who hear the preaching; but that only such are saved who actually believe.

4. How is this idea of the free offer of the gospel similar to a general promise?

Just as the free offer of the gospel expresses God's desire to save all men, so does a general promise; for a general promise to all means that God, on His part, promises to save all men.

5. Is a general promise even more serious than a free offer?

Although both are nearly the same, the free offer does not go as far as a general promise. In the free offer, God expresses a desire to save all; in a general promise, God actually promises to save all.

6. Are both the free offer and a general promise conditional?

Yes, for the free offer, while expressing God's desire to save all, teaches that only such as fulfill the condition of faith are actually saved. A general promise also teaches that only those who fulfill the condition of faith actually receive the promise.

7. Can the same objection be raised against the free offer as is raised against a general promise?

Yes, for both, in making faith a condition, also make faith the work of man. God, in the work of salvation, depends upon man's choice to believe.

8. What is another similarity?

Both speak of a certain common grace. Those who hold to a free offer believe that God gives grace to all who hear the gospel, by which grace every man is enabled to accept or reject Christ. While not all who hold to a general promise believe also in a certain common grace, some do. W. Heyns, long-time professor in Calvin College and Seminary in the earlier part of the 20th century, taught a "covenantal grace." All the children who are baptized receive this covenantal grace, whereby they are able to accept or reject the promise given to them in baptism.

9. Has history also proved that the two ideas are similar?

Yes, those in the Protestant Reformed Churches who held to conditional theology returned to the Christian Reformed Church after maintaining a separate existence for only a few years.

Conclusion

1. Did, then, the Protestant Reformed Churches fight to defend the same doctrines in 1953 which they fought to defend in 1924?

The issues were basically the same in both instances. The issues were the particularity of grace and the sovereign work of God in salvation.

2. Were the heresies promoted in 1953 a threat to the truth of Scripture and our Reformed confessions?

They were indeed. The false doctrines taught in the Protestant Reformed Churches were contrary to what the Reformed churches had maintained throughout their history from the time of the Reformation.

3. Were these heresies a threat to the very existence of the Protestant Reformed Churches?

Without question they were. Revs. H. Hoeksema, G. M. Ophoff, and H. Danhof had been expelled from the Christian Reformed Church because of their defense of sovereign and particular grace. The heresies of a general and conditional promise struck at the roots of all that the Protestant Reformed Churches had stood for in the years of their existence.

4. What would have happened if the Protestant Reformed Churches had adopted the views of those within their ranks who held to these heresies?

They would have denied all they had stood for since
the beginning of their existence and would have thereby
lost their right of existence.

**5.   Did God preserve the cause of His truth in the Protes-
tant Reformed Churches through this controversy?**
Even though more than half of the membership left
the Protestant Reformed Churches, God graciously preserved the denomination for a continued defense of the
truth.

**6.   Ought we, therefore, to be thankful for this contro-
versy?**
All glory belongs to God, who preserves His cause in
the midst of the world and makes His truth to triumph.

RELATED RFPA BOOKS

The complete history of the Protestant Reformed
Churches and of the struggles outlined in *Ready to Give an
Answer* can be found in *A Watered Garden: The History of
the Protestant Reformed Churches,* by Gertrude Hoeksema.

For fuller discussions of the doctrines of unconditional and particular grace and of the covenant of grace,
see Herman Hoeksema's *Believers and Their Seed* and
Whosoever Will, as well as Herman Hanko's *God's Everlasting Covenant of Grace.*

For further explanation of the Canons, see Homer C.
Hoeksema's exposition of the Canons of Dordt, *Voice of
Our Fathers.* For further explanation of the Lord's Days,
see Herman Hoeksema's exposition of the Heidelberg
Catechism, *The Triple Knowledge.*

Appendix

A BRIEF
DECLARATION OF PRINCIPLES
of the
PROTESTANT REFORMED CHURCHES

Preamble

DECLARATION OF PRINCIPLES, *to be used only by the Mission Committee and the missionaries for the organization of prospective churches on the basis of Scripture and the confessions as these have always been maintained in the Protestant Reformed Churches and as these are now further explained in regard to certain principles.*

The Protestant Reformed Churches stand on the basis of Scripture as the infallible Word of God and of the three forms of unity. Moreover, they accept the liturgical forms used in the public worship of our churches, such as:

Form for the Administration of Baptism, Form for the Administration of the Lord's Supper, Form of Excommunication, Form of Readmitting Excommunicated Persons, Form of Ordination of the Ministers of God's Word, Form of Ordination of Elders and Deacons, Form for the Installation of Professors of Theology, Form of Ordination of Missionaries, Form for the Confirmation of Marriage Before the Church, and the Formula of Subscription.

On the basis of this Word of God and these confessions:

I.   They repudiate the errors of the Three Points adopted

by the Synod of the Christian Reformed Church of Kalamazoo, 1924, which maintain:

A. That there is a grace of God to all men, including the reprobate, manifest in the common gifts to all men.

B. That the preaching of the gospel is a gracious offer of salvation on the part of God to all that externally hear the gospel.

C. That the natural man through the influence of common grace can do good in this world.

D. Over against this they maintain:

1. That the grace of God is always particular, i.e., only for the elect, never for the reprobate.

2. That the preaching of the gospel is not a gracious offer of salvation on the part of God to all men, nor a conditional offer to all that are born in the historical dispensation of the covenant, that is, to all that are baptized, but an oath of God that He will infallibly lead all the elect unto salvation and eternal glory through faith.

3. That the unregenerate man is totally incapable of doing any good, wholly depraved, and therefore can only sin.

For proof we refer to Canons I, A, 6-8:

> Art. 6. That some receive the gift of faith from God, and others do not receive it proceeds from God's eternal decree, "For known unto God are all his works from the beginning of the world," (Acts 15:18). "Who worketh all things after the counsel of his will," (Eph. 1:11). According to which decree, he graciously softens the hearts of the elect, however obstinate, and inclines them to believe, while he leaves the non-elect in his just judgment to their own wickedness and obduracy. And herein is espe-

cially displayed the profound, the merciful, and at the same time the righteous discrimination between men, equally involved in ruin; or that decree of election and reprobation, revealed in the Word of God, which though men of perverse, impure, and unstable minds wrest to their own destruction, yet to holy and pious souls affords unspeakable consolation.

Art. 7. Election is the unchangeable purpose of God, whereby, before the foundation of the world, he hath out of mere grace, according to the sovereign good pleasure of his own will, chosen, from the whole human race, which had fallen through their own fault, from their primitive state of rectitude, into sin and destruction, a certain number of persons to redemption in Christ, whom he from eternity appointed the Mediator and Head of the elect, and the foundation of salvation.

This elect number, though by nature neither better nor more deserving than others, but with them involved in one common misery, God hath decreed to give to Christ, to be saved by him, and effectually to call and draw them to his communion by his Word and Spirit, to bestow upon them true faith, justification and sanctification; and having powerfully preserved them in the fellowship of his Son, finally, to glorify them for the demonstration of his mercy, and for the praise of his glorious grace; as it is written, "According as he hath chosen us in him, before the foundation of the world, that we should be holy, and without blame before him in love; having predestinated us unto the adoption of children by Jesus Christ to himself, according to the good pleasure of his will, to the

praise of the glory of his grace, wherein he hath
made us accepted in the beloved," (Eph. 1:4, 5,
6). And elsewhere: "Whom he did predestinate, them he also called; and whom he called,
them he also justified; and whom he justified,
them he also glorified (Rom. 8:30).

Art. 8. There are not various decrees of
election, but one and the same decree respect-
ing all those who shall be saved, both under the
Old and New Testament: since the Scripture
declares the good pleasure, purpose, and counsel of the divine will to be one, according to
which he hath chosen us from eternity, both to
grace and glory, to salvation and the way of
salvation, which he hath ordained that we
should walk therein.

Canons II, A, 5:

Art. 5. Moreover, the promise of the gospel
is, that whosoever believeth in Christ crucified,
shall not perish, but have everlasting life. This
promise, together with the command to repent
and believe, ought to be declared and published to all nations, and to all persons promiscuously and without distinction, to whom God
out of his good pleasure sends the gospel.

The Canons in II, 5 speak of the preaching of
the promise. It presents the promise, not as general, but as particular, i.e., as for believers, and,
therefore, for the elect. This *preaching* of the particular promise is promiscuous to all that hear the
gospel, with the *command,* not a condition, to
repent and believe.

Canons II, B, 6:

Art. 6. Who use the difference between mer-

iting and appropriating, to the end that they
may instill into the minds of the imprudent and
inexperienced this teaching that God, as far as
he is concerned, has been minded of applying to
all equally the benefits gained by the death of
Christ; but that, while some obtain the pardon
of sin and eternal life, and others do not, this
difference depends on their own free will, which
joins itself to the grace that is offered without
exception, and that it is not dependent on the
special gift of mercy, which powerfully works
in them, that they rather than others should
appropriate unto themselves this grace.   For
these, while they feign that they present this
distinction, in a sound sense, seek to instill into
the people the destructive poison of the Pelagian
errors.

For further proof we refer to the Heidelberg
Catechism III, 8 and XXXIII, 91:

Q. 8.   Are we then so corrupt that we are
wholly incapable of doing any good, and inclined to all wickedness?

Indeed we are; except we are regenerated by
the Spirit of God.

Q. 91. But what are good works?

Only those which proceed from a true faith,
are performed according to the law of God, and
to his glory; and not such as are founded on our
imaginations, or the institutions of men.

And also from the Belgic Confession, Art. XIV:

Art. XIV. We believe that God created man
out of the dust of the earth, and made and
formed him after his own image and likeness,
good, righteous, and holy, capable in all things

to will, agreeably to the will of God. But being in honor, he understood it not, neither knew his excellency, but willfully subjected himself to sin, and consequently to death, and the curse, giving ear to the words of the devil. For the commandment of life, which he had received, he transgressed; and by sin separated himself from God, who was his true life, having corrupted his whole nature; whereby he made himself liable to corporal and spiritual death. And being thus become wicked, perverse, and corrupt in all his ways, he hath lost all his excellent gifts, which he had received from God, and only retained a few remains thereof, which, however, are sufficient to leave man without excuse; for all the light which is in us is changed into darkness, as the Scriptures teach us, saying: The light shineth in darkness, and the darkness comprehendeth it not: where St. John calleth men darkness. Therefore we reject all that is taught repugnant to this, concerning the free will of man, since man is but a slave to sin; and has nothing of himself, unless it is given from heaven. For who may presume to boast, that he of himself can do any good, since Christ saith, No man can come to me, except the Father, which hath sent me, draw him? Who will glory in his own will, who understands, that to be carnally minded is enmity against God? Who can speak of his knowledge, since the natural man receiveth not the things of the Spirit of God? In short, who dare suggest any thought, since he knows that we are not sufficient of ourselves to think anything as of ourselves, but that our sufficiency is of God? And therefore what the apostle saith ought

justly to be held sure and firm, that God worketh
in us both to will and to do of his good pleasure.
For there is no will nor understanding, con-
formable to the divine will and understanding,
but what Christ hath wrought in man; which he
teaches us, when he saith, Without me ye can
do nothing.

Once more we refer to Canons III/IV, A, 1-4:

Art. 1. Man was originally formed after the
image of God. His understanding was adorned
with a true and saving knowledge of his Creator, and of spiritual things; his heart and will
were upright; all his affections pure; and the
whole man was holy; but revolting from God
by the instigation of the devil, and abusing the
freedom of his own will, he forfeited these
excellent gifts; and on the contrary entailed on
himself blindness of mind, horrible darkness,
vanity and perverseness of judgment, became
wicked, rebellious, and obdurate in heart and
will, and impure in his affections.

Art. 2. Man after the fall begat children in his
own likeness. A corrupt stock produced a
corrupt offspring. Hence all the posterity of
Adam, Christ only excepted, have derived corruption from their original parent, not by imi-
tation, as the Pelagians of old asserted, but by
the propagation of a vicious nature.

Art. 3. Therefore all men are conceived in sin,
and by nature children of wrath, incapable of
saving good, prone to evil, dead in sin, and in
bondage thereto; and, without the regenerating
grace of the Holy Spirit, they are neither able
nor willing to return to God, to reform the
depravity of their nature, nor to dispose them-

selves to reformation.

Art. 4. There remain, however, in man since the fall, the glimmerings of natural light, whereby he retains some knowledge of God, of natural things, and of the differences between for good and evil, and discovers some regard virtue, good order in society, and for maintaining an orderly external deportment. But so far is this light of nature from being sufficient to bring him to a saving knowledge of God, and to true conversion, that he is incapable of using it aright even in things natural and civil. Nay further, this light, such as it is, man in various ways renders wholly polluted, and holds it in unrighteousness, by doing which he becomes inexcusable before God.

II. They teach on the basis of the same confessions:

A. That election, which is the unconditional and unchangeable decree of God to redeem in Christ a certain number of persons, is the sole cause and fountain of all our salvation, whence flow all the gifts of grace, including faith. This is the plain teaching of our confessions in the Canons of Dordrecht, I, A, 6, 7. See above.

And in the Heidelberg Catechism XXI, 54, we read:

Q. 54. What believest thou concerning the "holy catholic church" of Christ?

That the Son of God, from the beginning to the end of the world, gathers, defends, and preserves to himself by his Spirit and word, out of the whole human race, a church chosen to everlasting life, agreeing in true faith; and that I am and for ever shall remain, a living member thereof.

This is also evident from the doctrinal part of the Form for the Administration of Baptism, where we read:

> For when we are baptized in the name of the Father, God the Father witnesseth and sealeth unto us that he doth make an eternal covenant of grace with us, and adopts us for his children and heirs, and therefore will provide us with every good thing, and avert all evil or turn it to our profit. And when we are baptized in the name of the Son, the Son sealeth unto us that he doth wash us in his blood from all our sins, incorporating us into the fellowship of his death and resurrection, so that we are freed from all our sins, and accounted righteous before God. In like manner, when we are baptized in the name of the Holy Ghost, the Holy Ghost assures us, by this holy sacrament, that he will dwell in us, and sanctify us to be members of Christ, applying unto us that which we have in Christ, namely, the washing away of our sins, and the daily renewing of our lives, till we shall finally be presented without spot or wrinkle among the assembly of the elect in life eternal.

B. That Christ died only for the elect and that the saving efficacy of the death of Christ extends to them only.

This is evident from the Canons, II, A, 8:

> Art. 8. For this was the sovereign counsel, and most gracious will and purpose of God the Father, that the quickening and saving efficacy of the most precious death of his Son should extend to all the elect, for bestowing upon them alone the gift of justifying faith, thereby to

bring them infallibly to salvation: that is, it was the will of God that Christ, by the blood of the cross, whereby he confirmed the new covenant, should effectually redeem out of every people, tribe, nation, and language, all those, and those only, who were from eternity chosen to salvation, and given to him by the Father; that he should confer upon them faith, which together with all the other saving gifts of the Holy Spirit, he purchased for them by his death; should purge them from all sin, both original and actual, whether committed before or after believing; and having faithfully preserved them even to the end, should at last bring them free from every spot and blemish to the enjoyment of glory in his own presence forever.

This article very clearly teaches:
1. That all the covenant blessings are for the elect alone.
2. That God's promise is unconditionally for them only: for God cannot promise what was not objectively merited by Christ.
3. That the promise of God bestows the objective right of salvation not upon all the children that are born under the historical dispensation of the covenant, that is, not upon all that are baptized, but only upon the spiritual seed.

This is also evident from other parts of our confessions, as, for instance:

Heidelberg Catechism XXV, 65, 66:

Q. 65. Since then we are made partakers of Christ and all his benefits by faith only, whence doth this faith proceed?

From the Holy Ghost, who works faith in our hearts by the preaching of the gospel, and confirms it by the use of the sacraments.

Q. 66. What are the sacraments?

The sacraments are holy visible signs and seals, appointed of God for this end, that by the use thereof, he may the more fully declare and seal to us the promise of the gospel, viz., that he grants us freely the remission of sin, and life eternal, for the sake of that one sacrifice of Christ accomplished on the cross.

If we compare with these statements from the Heidelberger what was taught concerning the saving efficacy of the death of Christ in Canons II, A, 8, it is evident that the promise of the gospel which is sealed by the sacraments concerns only the believers, that is, the elect.

This is also evident from Heidelberg Catechism XXVII, 74:

Q. 74. Are infants also to be baptized?

Yes: for since they, as well as the adult, are included in the covenant and church of God; and since redemption from sin by the blood of Christ, and the Holy Ghost, the author of faith, is promised to them no less than to the adult; they must therefore by baptism, as a sign of the covenant, be also admitted into the Christian church; and be distinguished from the children of unbelievers as was done in the old covenant or testament by circumcision, instead of which baptism is instituted in the new covenant.

That in this question and answer of the Heidelberger not all the children that are baptized, but only the spiritual children, that is, the elect, are meant is evident. For:

a. Little infants surely cannot fulfill any con-

ditions. And if the promise of God is for
them, the promise is infallible and unconditional, and therefore only for the elect.

b. According to Canons II, A, 8, which we
quoted above, the saving efficacy of the
death of Christ is for the elect alone.

c. According to this answer of the Heidelberg
Catechism, the Holy Ghost, the author of
faith, is promised to the little children no
less than to the adult. And God surely
fulfills His promise. Hence, that promise is
surely only for the elect.

The same is taught in the Belgic Confession, Articles XXXIII-XXXV. In Article
XXXIII we read:

> Art. XXXIII. We believe, that our gra-
> cious God, on account of our weakness and
> infirmities hath ordained the sacraments
> for us, thereby to seal unto us his promises,
> and to be pledges of the good will and grace
> of God toward us, and also to nourish and
> strengthen our faith; which he hath joined
> to the Word of the gospel, the better to
> present to our senses, both that which he
> signifies to us by his Word, and that which
> he works inwardly in our hearts, thereby
> assuring and confirming in us the salvation
> which he imparts to us. For they are visible
> signs and seals of an inward and invisible
> thing, by means whereof God worketh in
> us by the power of the Holy Ghost. There-
> fore the signs are not in vain or insignifi-
> cant, so as to deceive us. For Jesus Christ is
> the true object presented by them, without
> whom they would be of no moment.

And from Article XXXIV, which speaks of holy baptism, we quote:

Art. XXXIV. We believe and confess that Jesus Christ, who is the end of the law, hath made an end, by the shedding of his blood, of all other sheddings of blood which men could or would make as a propitiation or satisfaction for sin: and that he, having abolished circumcision, which was done with blood, hath instituted the sacrament of baptism instead thereof; by which we are received into the church of God, and separated from all other people and strange religions, that we may wholly belong to him, whose ensign and banner we bear: and which serves as a testimony to us, that he will forever be our gracious God and Father.   Therefore he has commanded all those, who are his, to be baptized with pure water, "in the name of the Father, and of the Son, and of the Holy Ghost"; thereby signifying to us, that as water washeth away the filth of the body, when poured upon it, and is seen on the body of the baptized, when sprinkled upon him; so doth the blood of Christ, by the power of the Holy Ghost, internally sprinkle the soul, cleanse it from its sins, and regenerate us from children of wrath unto children of God. Not that this is effected by the external water, but by the sprinkling of the precious blood of the Son of God; who is our Red Sea, through which we must pass, to escape the tyranny of Pharaoh, that is, the devil, and to enter into the spiritual land of Canaan. Therefore the

ministers, on their part, administer the sacrament, and that which is visible, but our
Lord giveth that which is signified by the
sacrament, namely, the gifts and invisible
grace; washing, cleansing, and purging our
souls of all filth and unrighteousness; renewing our hearts, and filling them with all
comfort; giving unto us a true assurance of
his fatherly goodness; putting on us the
new man, and putting off the old man with
all his deeds.

Article XXXIV speaks of holy baptism.
That all this, washing and cleansing and
purging our souls of all filth and
unrighteousness, the renewal of our hearts,
is only the fruit of the saving efficacy of the
death of Christ and therefore is only for the
elect is very evident. The same is true of
what we read in the same article concerning the baptism of infants:

Art. XXXIV. And indeed Christ shed his
blood no less for the washing of the children of the faithful, than for adult persons;
and therefore they ought to receive the sign
and sacrament of that, which Christ hath
done for them; as the Lord commanded in
the law, that they should be made partakers of the sacrament of Christ's suffering
and death, shortly after they were born, by
offering for them a lamb, which was a
sacrament of Jesus Christ. Moreover, what
circumcision was to the Jews, that baptism
is to our children. And for this reason Paul
calls baptism the circumcision of Christ.

If, according to Article 8 of the Second Head of Doctrine, A, in the Canons, the saving efficacy of the death of Christ extends only to the elect, it follows that when in this article of the Belgic Confession it is stated that "Christ shed his blood no less for the washing of the children of the faithful than for the adult persons," also here the reference is only to the elect children.

Moreover, that the promise of the gospel which God signifies and seals in the sacraments is not for all is also abundantly evident from Article XXXV of the same Belgic Confession, which speaks of the holy supper of our Lord Jesus Christ. For there we read:

Art. XXXV. We believe and confess, that our Savior Jesus Christ did ordain and institute the sacrament of the holy supper, to nourish and support those whom he hath already regenerated, and incorporated into his family, which is his church.

In the same article we read:

Further, though the sacraments are connected with the thing signified, nevertheless both are not received by all men: the ungodly indeed receives the sacrament to his condemnation, but he doth not receive the truth of the sacrament. As Judas, and Simon the sorcerer, both indeed received the sacrament, but not Christ who was signified by it, of whom believers only are made partakers.

It follows from this that both the sacraments, as well as the preaching of the gospel, are a savor of death unto death for the reprobate, as well as a savor of life unto life for the elect. Hence, the promise of God, preached by the gospel, signified and sealed in both the sacraments, is not for all but for the elect only.

And that the election of God, and consequently the efficacy of the death of Christ and the promise of the gospel, is not conditional is abundantly evident from the following articles of the Canons.

Canons I, A, 10:

Art 10. The good pleasure of God is the sole cause of this gracious election; which doth not consist herein, that out of all possible qualities and actions of men God has chosen some as a condition of salvation; but that he was pleased out of the common mass of sinners to adopt some certain persons as a peculiar people to himself, as it is written, "For the children being not yet born neither having done any good or evil," etc., it was said (namely to Rebecca): "the elder shall serve the younger; as it is written, Jacob have I loved, but Esau have I hated," (Rom. 9:11, 12, 13). "And as many as were ordained to eternal life believed" (Acts 13:48).

In Canons I, B, 2, the errors are repudiated of those who teach:

Art. 2. That there are various kinds of election of God unto eternal life: the one general and indefinite, the other particular and definite; and that the latter in turn is either incomplete, revocable, non-decisive and conditional, or complete, irrevocable, decisive, and absolute....

And in the same chapter of Canons I, B, 3, the errors are repudiated of those who teach:

Art. 3. That the good pleasure and purpose of God, of which Scripture makes mention in the doctrine of election, does not consist in this, that God chose certain persons rather than others, but in this that he chose out of all possible conditions (among which are also the works of the law), or out of the whole order of things, the act of faith which from its very nature is undeserving, as well as its incomplete obedience, as a condition of salvation, and that he would graciously consider this in itself as a complete obedience and count it worthy of the reward of eternal life....

Again, in the same chapter of Canons I, B, 5, the errors are rejected of those who teach that:

Art. 5. ... faith, the obedience of faith, holiness, godliness and perseverance are not fruits of the unchangeable election unto glory, but are conditions, which, being required beforehand, were foreseen as being met by those who will be fully elected, and are causes without which the unchangeable election to glory does not occur.

Finally, we refer to the statement of the

baptism form:

> And although our young children do not
> understand these things, we may not there-
> fore exclude them from baptism, for as they
> are without their knowledge partakers of
> the condemnation in Adam, so are they
> again received unto grace in Christ....

That here none other than the elect children of the covenant are meant and that
they are unconditionally, without their
knowledge, received unto grace in Christ,
in the same way as they are under the
condemnation of Adam, is very evident.

C. That faith is not a prerequisite or condition unto
salvation, but a gift of God, and a God-given
instrument whereby we appropriate the salvation
in Christ. This is plainly taught in the following
parts of our confessions:

Heidelberg Catechism VII, 20:

> Q. 20. Are all men then, as they perished in
> Adam, saved by Christ?
> No; only those who are ingrafted into him, and
> receive all his benefits, by a true faith.

Belgic Confession, Article XXII:

> Art. XXII. We believe that, to attain the true
> knowledge of this great mystery, the Holy Ghost
> kindleth in our hearts an upright faith, which em-
> braces Jesus Christ, with all his merits, appropri-
> ates him, and seeks nothing more besides him. For
> it must needs follow, either that all things, which
> are requisite to our salvation, are not in Jesus
> Christ, or if all things are in him, that then those
> who possess Jesus Christ through faith, have com-
> plete salvation in him. Therefore, for any to assert,

that Christ is not sufficient, but that something more is required besides him, would be too gross a blasphemy: for hence it would follow, that Christ was but half a Savior. Therefore we justly say with Paul, that we are justified by faith alone, or by faith without works. However, to speak more clearly, we do not mean, that faith itself justifies us, for it is only an instrument with which we embrace Christ our Righteousness. But Jesus Christ, imputing to us all his merits, and so many holy works which he has done for us, and in our stead, is our Righteousness. And faith is an instrument that keeps us in communion with him in all his benefits, which, when become ours, are more than sufficient to acquit us of our sins.

Confer also Belgic Confession, Articles XXXIII-XXXV, quoted above (see pp. 214-216).

In Canons III/IV, A, 10, 14 we read:

Art. 10. But that others who are called by the gospel, obey the call, and are converted, is not to be ascribed to the proper exercise of free will, whereby one distinguishes himself above others, equally furnished with grace sufficient for faith and conversions, as the proud heresy of Pelagius maintains; but it must be wholly ascribed to God, who as he has chosen his own from eternity in Christ, so he confers upon them faith and repentance, rescues them from the power of darkness, and translates them into the kingdom of his own Son, that they may show forth the praises of him, who hath called them out of darkness into his marvelous light; and may glory not in themselves, but in the Lord according to the testimony of the apostles in various places.

Again, in the same chapter of Canons, Article 14, we read:

> Art. 14. Faith is therefore to be considered as the gift of God, not on account of its being offered by God to man, to be accepted or rejected at his pleasure; but because it is in reality conferred, breathed, and infused into him; or even because God bestows the power or ability to believe, and then expects that man should by the exercise of his own free will, consent to the terms of salvation, and actually believe in Christ; but because he who works in man both to will and to do, and indeed all things in all, produces both the will to believe, and the act of believing also.

III. Seeing then that this is the clear teaching of our confession,
   A. We repudiate:
     1. The teaching:
       a. That the promise of the covenant is conditional and for all that are baptized.
       b. That we may presuppose that all the children that are baptized are regenerated, for we know on the basis of Scripture, as well as in the light of all history and experience, that the contrary is true.

        For proof we refer to Canons I, A, 6-8; and the doctrinal part of the baptismal form:

> The principal parts of the doctrine of holy baptism are these three:
> First. That we with our children are conceived and born in sin, and therefore are children of wrath, in so much that we cannot enter into the kingdom of God ex-

cept we are born again. This, the dipping
in, or sprinkling with water teaches us,
whereby the impurity of our souls is signified, and we admonished to loathe and
humble ourselves before God, and seek for
our purification and salvation without ourselves.

Secondly. Holy baptism witnesseth and
sealeth unto us the washing away of our
sins through Jesus Christ. Therefore we are
baptized in the name of the Father, and of
the Son, and of the Holy Ghost. For when
we are baptized in the name of the Father,
God the Father witnesseth and sealeth unto
us the washing away of our sins through
Jesus Christ. Therefore we are baptized in
the name of the Father, and of the Son, and
of the Holy Ghost. For when we are baptized in the name of the Father, God the
Father witnesseth and sealeth unto us that
he doth make an eternal covenant of grace
with us, and adopts us for his children and
heirs, and therefore will provide us with
every good thing, and avert all evil or turn
it to our profit. And when we are baptized
in the name of the Son, the Son sealeth unto
us that he doth wash us in his blood from all
our sins, incorporating us into the fellowship of his death and resurrection, so that
we are freed from all our sins, and accounted righteous before God. In like manner, when we are baptized in the name of
the Holy Ghost, the Holy Ghost assures us,
by this holy sacrament, that he will dwell in
us, and sanctify us to be members of Christ,
applying unto us that which we have in

Christ, namely, the washing away of our sins, and the daily renewing of our lives, till we shall finally be presented without spot or wrinkle among the assembly of the elect in life eternal.

Thirdly. Whereas in all covenants there are contained two parts: therefore are we by God through baptism admonished of and obliged unto new obedience, namely, that we cleave to this one God, Father, Son, and Holy Ghost; that we trust in him, and love him with all our hearts, with all our souls, with all our mind, and with all our strength; that we forsake the world, crucify our old nature, and walk in a new and holy life.

And if we sometimes through weakness fall into sin, we must not therefore despair of God's mercy, nor continue in sin, since baptism is a seal and undoubted testimony that we have an eternal covenant of grace with God.

The Thanksgiving after baptism:

Almighty God and merciful Father, we thank and praise thee that thou hast forgiven us and our children all our sins, through the blood of thy beloved Son Jesus Christ, and received us through thy Holy Spirit as members of thine only begotten Son, and adopted us to be thy children, and sealed and confirmed the same unto us by holy baptism; we beseech thee, through the same Son of thy love, that thou wilt be pleased always to govern these baptized children by thy Holy Spirit, that they may be piously and religiously educated, increase and grow up in the Lord Jesus Christ, that they then may acknowledge thy fatherly goodness and mercy, which thou hast shown to them and us, and live in all righteousness, under our only Teacher, King, and High Priest, Jesus Christ; and manfully fight against and overcome sin, the devil, and his whole dominion, to the end that they may eternally praise and magnify thee, and thy Son Jesus Christ, together with the Holy Ghost, the one only true God. Amen.

The prayer refers only to the elect; we cannot presuppose that it is for all.

2. The teaching that the promise of the covenant is an objective bequest on the part of God, giving to every baptized child the right to Christ and all the blessings of salvation.

B. And we maintain:

1. That God surely and infallibly fulfills His promise to the elect.

2. The sure promise of God which He realizes in us as rational and moral creatures not only makes it impossible that we should not bring forth fruits of thankfulness but also confronts us with the obligation of love, to walk in a new and holy life, and constantly to watch unto prayer.

All those who are not thus disposed, who do not repent but walk in sin, are the objects of His just wrath and excluded from the kingdom of heaven.

That the preaching comes to all; and that God seriously commands to faith and repentance; and that to all those who come and believe He promises life and peace.

Grounds:

a. The baptism form, part 3.

b. The form for the Lord's Supper, under "thirdly":

All those, then, who are thus disposed, God will certainly receive in mercy, and count them worthy partakers of the table of his Son Jesus Christ. On the contrary, those who do not feel this testimony in their hearts eat and drink judgment to themselves.

Therefore, we also, according to the command of Christ and the apostle Paul, admonish all those who are defiled with the following sins to keep themselves from the table of the Lord, and declare to them that they have no part in the kingdom of Christ; such as all idolaters, all those who invoke deceased saints, angels, or other creatures; all those who worship images; all enchanters, diviners, charmers, and those who confide in such enchantments; all despisers of God, and of his Word, and of the holy sacraments; all blasphemers; all those who are given to raise discord, sects, and mutiny in church or state; all perjured persons; all those who are disobedient to their parents and superiors; all murderers, contentious persons, and those who live in hatred and envy against their neighbors; all adulterers, whoremongers, drunkards, thieves, usurers, robbers, gamesters, covetous, and all who lead offensive lives.

All these, while they continue in such sins, shall abstain from this meat (which Christ hath ordained only for the faithful), lest their judgment and condemnation be made the heavier.

c.   The Heidelberg Catechism XXIV, 64; XXXI, 84; XLV, 116:

Q. 64. But doth not this doctrine make men careless and profane?

By no means: for it is impossible that those, who are implanted into Christ by a true faith, should not bring forth fruits of thankfulness.

Q. 84. How is the kingdom of heaven opened and shut by the preaching of the holy gospel?

Thus: when according to the command of Christ, it is declared and publicly testified to all and every believer, that, whenever they receive the promise of the gospel by a true faith, all their sins are really forgiven them of God, for the sake of Christ's merits; and on the contrary, when it is declared and testified to all unbelievers, and such as do not sincerely repent, that they stand exposed to the wrath of God, and eternal condemnation, so long as they are unconverted: according to which testimony of the gospel, God will judge them, both in this, and in the life to come.

Q. 116. Why is prayer necessary for Christians?

Because it is the chief part of thankfulness which God requires of us: and also, because God will give his grace and Holy Spirit to those only, who with sincere desires continually ask them of him, and are thankful for them.

Canons III/IV, A, 12, 16, 17:

Art. 12. And this is the regeneration so highly celebrated in Scripture, and denominated a new creation: a resurrection from the dead, a making alive, which God works in us without our aid. But this is in no wise effected merely by the external preaching of the gospel, by moral suasion, or such a mode of operation, that after God has performed his part, it still remains in the power of man to be regenerated or not, to be converted, or to continue unconverted; but it is evidently a supernatural work, most powerful, and at the same time most delightful, astonishing, mysterious, and ineffable; not inferior in efficacy to creation, or the resurrection from the dead, as the Scripture inspired by the author of this work declares; so that all in whose heart God works in this marvelous manner, are certainly, infallibly, and effectually regenerated, and do actually believe—Whereupon the will thus renewed, is not only actuated and influenced by God, but in consequence of this influence, becomes itself active. Wherefore also, man is himself rightly said to believe and repent, by virtue of that grace received.

Art. 16. But as man by the fall did not cease to be a creature, endowed with understanding and will, nor did sin which pervaded the whole race of mankind, deprive him of the human nature, but brought upon him depravity and spiritual death; so also this grace of regeneration does not treat men as senseless stocks and blocks, nor takes away their will and its properties, neither does violence thereto; but spiritually quickens, heals, corrects, and at the same time sweetly and powerfully bends it; that where carnal rebellion and resistance formerly prevailed, a ready and sincere spiritual obedience begins to reign; in which the true and spiritual restoration and freedom of our will consist. Wherefore unless the admirable author of every good work wrought in us, man could have no hope of recovering from his fall by his own free will, by the abuse of which, in a state of innocence, he plunged himself into ruin.

Art. 17. As the almighty operation of God, whereby he prolongs and supports this our natural life, does not exclude, but requires the use of means, by which God of his infinite mercy and goodness hath chosen to exert his influence, so also the before mentioned supernatural operation of God, by which we are regenerated, in no wise excludes, or subverts the use of the gospel, which the most wise God has ordained to be the seed of regeneration, and food of the soul. Wherefore, as the apostles, and teachers who succeeded them, piously instructed the people concerning this grace, of God, to his glory, and the abasement of all pride, and in the meantime, however, neglected not to keep them by the sacred precepts of the gospel in the exercise of the Word, sacraments, and discipline; so even to this day, be it far from either instructors or instructed to presume to tempt God in the church by separating what he of his good pleasure hath most intimately joined together. For grace is conferred by means of admonitions; and the more readily we perform our duty, the more eminent usually is this blessing of God working in us, and the more directly is his work advanced; to whom alone all the glory both of means and of their saving fruit and efficacy is forever due. Amen.

Canons III/IV, B, 9:

Art. 9. Who teach: That grace and free will are partial causes, which together work the beginning of conversion, and that grace, in order of working, does not precede the working of the will; that is, that God does not efficiently help the will of man unto conversion until the will of man moves and determines to do this. For the ancient church has long ago condemned this doctrine of the Pelagians according to the words of the apostle: "So then it is not of him that willeth, nor of him that runneth, but of God that sheweth mercy" (Rom. 9:16). Likewise: "For who maketh thee to differ? and what hast thou that thou didst not receive?" (I Cor. 4:7). And: "For it is God who worketh in you both to will and to do of his good pleasure" (Phil. 2:13).

Canons V, A, 14:

Art. 14. And as it hath pleased God, by the preaching of the gospel, to begin this work of grace in us, so he preserves, continues, and perfects it by the hearing and reading of his Word, by meditation thereon, and by the exhortations, threatenings, and promises thereof, as well as by the use of the sacraments.

Belgic Confession, Article XXIV:

Art. XXIV. We believe that this true faith being wrought in man by the hearing of the Word of God, and the operation of the Holy Ghost, doth regenerate and make him a new man, causing him to live a new life, and freeing him from the bondage of sin. Therefore it is so far from being true, that this justifying faith makes men remiss in a pious and holy life, that on the contrary without it they would never do anything out of love to God, but only out of self-love or fear of damnation. Therefore it is impossible that this holy faith can be unfruitful in man: for we do not speak of a vain faith, but of such a faith, which is called in Scripture a faith that worketh by love, which excites man to the practice of those works, which God has commanded in his Word.

Which works, as they proceed from the good root of faith, are good and acceptable in the sight of God, forasmuch as they are all sanctified by His grace: howbeit they are of no account towards our justification. For it is by faith in Christ that we are justified, even before we do good works; otherwise they could not be good works, any more than the fruit of a tree can be good, before the tree itself is good.

Therefore we do good works, but not to merit by them, (for what can we merit?), nay, we are beholden to God for the good works we do, and not he to us, since it is he that worketh in us both to will and to do of his good pleasure. Let us therefore attend to what is written: When ye shall have done all those things which are commanded you, say, we are unprofitable servants; we have done that which was our duty to do. In the meantime, we do not deny that God rewards our good works, but it is through his grace that he crowns his gifts.

Moreover, though we do good works, we do not found our salvation upon them; for we do no work but what is polluted by our flesh, and also punishable; and although we could perform such works, still the remembrance of one sin is sufficient to make God reject them. Thus

then we would always be in doubt, tossed to
and fro without any certainty, and our poor
consciences continually vexed, if they relied
not on the merits of the suffering and death of
our Savior.

3. That the ground of infant baptism is the command of God and the fact that according to
   Scripture He established His covenant in the
   line of continued generations.

IV. Besides, the Protestant Reformed Churches:
Believe and maintain the autonomy of the local church.
For proof we refer to the Belgic Confession, Article
XXXI:

Art. XXXI. We believe that the ministers of God's
Word, and the elders and deacons, ought to be chosen
to their respective offices by a lawful election by the
church, with calling upon the name of the Lord, and in
that order which the Word of God teacheth. Therefore
everyone must take heed not to intrude himself by
indecent means, but is bound to wait till it shall please
God to call him; that he may have testimony of his
calling, and be certain and assured that it is of the Lord.
As for the ministers of God's Word, they have equally
the same power and authority wheresoever they are, as
they are all ministers of Christ, the only universal
Bishop, and the only Head of the church. Moreover,
that this holy ordinance of God may not be violated or
slighted, we say that every one ought to esteem the
ministers of God's Word, and the elders of the church,
very highly for their work's sake, and be at peace with
them without murmuring, strife or contention, as much
as possible.

Church Order, Article 36:

Art. 36. The classis has the same jurisdiction over the consistory as the particular synod has over the classis and the general synod over the particular.

Only the consistory has authority over the local congregation. Church Order, Article 84:

Art. 84. No church shall in any way lord it over other churches, no minister over other ministers, no elder or deacon over other elders or deacons.

The Form for the Installation of Elders and Deacons:

"... called of God's church, and consequently of God himself...."

Scriptural Index

Creedal Index

Other RFPA books in print
... by Herman Hoeksema

Believers and Their Seed, Children in the Covenant
A clear and concise exposition of the biblical teaching of God's covenant of grace. Such important topics as the relation of infant baptism to the covenant, the place of believers in the covenant, and the salvation of children of believers who die in infancy are treated.

Behold He Cometh
One of the few commentaries on the book of Revelation by a Reformed theologian. The amillennial viewpoint is Reformed in character and always ascribes all the glory to God.

In The Sanctuary
Using the Lord's Prayer as the perfect model of intercession and fellowship with the Father, this book discusses true prayer.

The Mystery of Bethlehem
Enjoy Hoeksema's flowing style in this devotional on the wonder of Christ's birth, which emphasizes the *mystery* of the events at Bethlehem.

The Triple Knowledge
The most extensive commentary on the Heidelberg Catechism in the English language. It is a thorough explanation, in three volumes, of the fifty-two Lord's Days which will help the reader grow in his understanding of his sin, salvation, and thankful service.

When I Survey

A Lenten anthology focusing on the cross, written in simple, easy-to-read language, but profound in thought. The believing reader will find his eyes fixed on that cross, in sorrow for sin, and in love for the Savior who died for him there.

"Whosoever Will"

The author makes clear from Scripture that these words, so often quoted and sung, have a far deeper and richer meaning than they are usually given.

Wonder of Grace

A fresh approach from Scripture to the truth that salvation is of God alone, all the while stressing grace as a *wonder*.

... and by Herman Hanko

Far Above Rubies

This book, edited by Herman Hanko, is a series of essays written by different authors, which point the reader to God's Word to discover the biblical and Reformed definition of a Christian woman's place in the home as wife and mother, in the church as believer, and in her calling in God's covenant.

God's Everlasting Covenant of Grace

This book examines Scripture's teaching on the doctrine of the covenant from the viewpoint of the historical narrative, beginning with the creation of man, through the line of God's covenant with His people in the Old Testament until the time of the fulfillment of the covenant in Christ. The richness and warmth of God's covenant comes through in this biblical exposition of a central doctrine of Scripture.

The Mysteries of the Kingdom

This treatment of the parables in chronological order will draw the student of Scripture back to the parables again and again to search their depth of meaning. The focus of the book on the principles of the kingdom of heaven as they apply to the calling of the citizens of that kingdom is a benefit to all who read it.

We and Our Children

The arguments of those who reject infant baptism need answering. This book demonstrates from the Scriptures, in answer to the stated position of Reformed Baptists, that the practice of infant baptism is not only consistent with but required by the doctrines of the Reformed faith.